Teaching Science, Design and Technology in the Early Years

DD – to Peter and Beryl, who gave me a carpentry set for my seventh birthday

AH – to Mum and Dad – my first science and design & technology teachers

Teaching Science, Design and Technology in the Early Years

Dan Davies & Alan Howe

David Fulton Publishers
London

David Fulton Publishers Ltd
The Chiswick Centre, 414 Chiswick High Road, London W4 5TF
www.fultonpublishers.co.uk

Copyright © David Fulton Publishers 2003
Reprinted 2003
10 9 8 7 6 5 4 3 2

British Library Cataloguing in Publication Data
A catalogue record for this book is available from the British Library.

ISBN 1 85346 880 0

Typeset by Servis Filmsetting Ltd, Manchester
Printed and bound in Scotland by Scotprint, Haddington Scotland

Contents

Notes on the authors and contributors

Dan Davies is Senior Lecturer in Primary Science and D&T at Bath Spa University College. He has taught the 4 to 7 age range in London primary schools and has published widely in the fields of primary science and D&T education, including *Primary Design and Technology for the Future*, published by David Fulton.

Alan Howe is also Senior Lecturer in Primary Science and D&T at Bath Spa University College. He has taught in a number of primary schools and has published in the field of primary D&T education, including *Primary Design and Technology for the Future*, published by David Fulton.

Pat Black is Senior Lecturer in Primary English and Early Years at Bath Spa University College. She has taught the 4 to 7 age range in a South Gloucestershire primary school and is co-author of a maths programme for Reception/P1 called *Platform One*, published by Stanley Thornes.

Sue Hughes is Senior Lecturer in Primary and Middle English at Bath Spa University College. She has taught across the primary age range in Bristol primary schools and in her role as literacy consultant has developed training and resource materials for subject specific and cross-curricular literacy in both Foundation Stage and Key Stage 1.

Karen McInnes is a lecturer in Early Years education at Bath Spa University College. She has taught the 3 to 7 age range in primary schools in London and Bristol. She has been a science co-ordinator and an Early Years co-ordinator. She has conducted and published research on 4-year-olds.

Kendra McMahon is Senior Lecturer in Primary Science Education at Bath Spa University College. She was formerly deputy head teacher of a primary school in South Gloucestershire and is a member of the national primary committee for the Association for Science Education (ASE). She has published in the field of primary science education, including *100 Science Lessons: Year 4*, published by Scholastic.

Tonie Scott is Deputy Head Teacher and Reception class teacher at Bishop Henderson Primary School, Coleford, Somerset and has been teaching young children for 17 years. She has worked closely with Sandy Sheppard on Foundation Stage in-service training and has also worked with PGCE students on the science and D&T elements of their courses.

Sandy Sheppard has been teaching children in the Early Years for 15 years, and is currently the nursery class teacher and Foundation Stage co-ordinator at Bishop Henderson Primary. She has led many maths and science workshops for Foundation Stage colleagues and pre-school groups and run several Early Years science workshops at regional ASE conferences.

Stephen Ward is Head of Education and Childhood Studies at Bath Spa University College. He has taught the 4 to 7 age range in primary schools in Leeds and has published in the fields of the primary curriculum, primary music and teacher education.

Jill Williams is a Senior Lecturer in Early Years education at Bath Spa University College. She has a strong interest in a creative approach to teaching and learning. Jill has travelled widely and has observed and recorded children in many cultural contexts. She has written a book to be published by the Open University Press concerning children and independence.

Acknowledgements

Alison Howe, other staff and children at St Philips CE Primary School, Bath

Alison Stubbs, other staff and children at Moorlands Infant School, Bath

Angela Tipping, other staff and children at Bowsland Green County Primary School, South Gloucestershire

Angela Millar, other staff and children at Oak Tree Day Nursery, Bath

Di Rhodes and Margaret Harrison, other staff and children at Newbridge St John CE Infants School, Bath

John Paul Sharman

Judy Cooper, Mandi Macey, other staff and children at Broad Chalke CE First School, Wiltshire

Julia Sutcliffe, Old Sodbury CE VC Primary School, South Gloucestershire

Louise Hern

Mo Pearson, other staff and children at Blaise Primary School and Nursery, Bristol

Moira Hill, Elm Park Primary School, South Gloucestershire

Sarah Stillie, Bromley Heath County Infants School, South Gloucestershire

Sue Hunt, other staff and children at Filton Hill Primary School, Bristol

CHAPTER 1

Introduction

Dan Davies

Purpose of this chapter

Through reading this chapter, you should gain

- an introduction to our philosophy of Early Years education
- an understanding of the ways in which we see science and D&T as relevant to the education of young children
- an appreciation of the structure and contents of this book.

This book is the result of collaboration between Early Years educators and tutors at Bath Spa University College. We write not out of a desire to see science and design & technology (D&T) 'taught' to young children, but from a concern for a holistic approach to Early Years provision. Our use of the terms 'holistic' and 'holism' in this book refers to the whole child – cognitive, physical, emotional and spiritual. Every aspect of young children's development needs to be provided for in the various settings in which they are educated – home, childminder's home, playgroup, day nursery, school – and this includes the sometimes overlooked elements of scientific, designerly and technological development. In the chapters that follow we will make explicit these aspects of young children's holistic learning and provide guidance on assessing, planning for and intervening in Early Years science and D&T. Before we begin, however, it is necessary to define more precisely the phase of education and areas of experience to which the title of this book refers.

What do we mean by the Early Years?

In this book we will take the phrase 'Early Years' to refer to children aged between 3 and 7, i.e. from the start of nursery education to the end of Key Stage 1 in England and correlating to the proposed statutory Foundation Phase in Wales (National Assembly for Wales 2001). We have taken this decision for two main reasons:

1. At the age of 3, many children in England and Wales have their first taste of an educational setting outside the home; it is at this point that we can begin to share

our understandings and offer advice for enriching children's scientific, designerly and technological experiences. Some would argue that the Early Years start from birth, or even conception. We would certainly agree that children have experiences before the age of 3 that relate to science and D&T, such as bath-time, exploring the tactile properties of toys or changing the shape of playdough, but the opportunities for adults to intervene in this process are more limited.

Children between the ages of 5 and 7 need the kinds of exploratory, contextualised, meaningful activities characteristic of good practice in Nursery and Reception classes. They are, in our opinion, in their Early Years. For some, the Early Years come to an end when children enter compulsory education, and UK government curriculum guidance for nursery education has come to be seen as the 'Early Years curriculum'. In 1996 the Schools Curriculum and Assessment Authority (SCAA) issued non-statutory guidance in the form of *Desirable Outcomes for Children's Learning on Entering Compulsory Education*. Following consultation, these were revised as *Curriculum Guidance for the Foundation Stage* (QCA/DfEE 2000) and in Wales the *Desirable Outcomes for Children's Learning before Compulsory School Age* (ACCAC 2000)

2. The establishment of a new 'Key Stage' in the education system – albeit a non-statutory one in England – preceding Key Stage 1 (5–7 years), with the word 'early' in its assessment framework, seems to imply that this is the official definition of the Early Years. There are signs that Key Stage 1 has become more formal in recent years, with the introduction of the National Literacy and Numeracy Strategies (DfEE 1998a, 1999) and an increased emphasis upon whole-class teaching. Yet in several countries – Sweden for example – children do not *begin* statutory schooling until they are 7 (i.e. at the end of Key Stage 1) and in others (USA, Finland, Australia) the years from 5 to 7 are described as kindergarten – 'children's garden' – implying an educational ethos more akin to that of nursery education in the UK. In Piagetian terms, children in these age groups are working within a 'pre-operational' phase of cognitive development, and even if we accept that they are capable of more abstract thinking within meaningful contexts (Donaldson 1978) it can be argued that a child of 7 has more in common with a 3-year-old than an 11-year-old.

We therefore strongly reject the equating of Early Years with the Foundation Stage in England and support the Welsh position. Excellent Early Years practice should continue throughout Key Stage 1 and beyond. Characteristics of such practice include a concern for the 'whole child'; the fostering of independence through self-directed activities; attention to issues of inclusion; and the primacy of narrative and verbal interaction in the interventions adults make in children's learning.

Why science in the Early Years?

Science begins with children's very first acts of exploration.

(de Boo 2000: 1)

Science is not a 'subject' in the Foundation Stage curriculum for England. Indeed, until comparatively recently, the term did not feature in primary education at all and is still absent from the elementary curricula of many countries. This is not to say that science was not, or is not, happening in nurseries, infant classes, playgroups and childminders' and children's homes. Many activities in which young children spontaneously engage are intrinsically scientific, or can be made to be so: blowing bubbles, playing with sand and water, looking at flowers or spiders' webs. There are, however, major problems of *definition* and *recognition*. As practitioners, our definitions of science are often too narrow, resulting in an inability to recognise where it is going on.

The images we have of science in the world beyond the classroom will inevitably affect our attitude towards children's scientific activity, and will in turn be transmitted to the children with whom we work (Harlen 2000). A multiplicity of meanings surround the word 'science' in general use:

> Science . . . can mean organised knowledge about natural phenomena ('Einstein's theory of relativity was a major contribution to science'), or the thought processes which generate such knowledge ('Discovering the structure of DNA was a triumph of modern science') or as a rubric for a set of disciplines ('Psychology as a science is a century old'); it can also refer to social systems and fields of work and study.
>
> (Gardner 1994: 2)

If, from our own educational experience, we see science as a factual body of knowledge about the world, concerned with laws and formulae and 'discovered' through complex experiments, we will find it difficult to recognise the scientific significance of four-year-olds pushing each other around on wheeled toys. If, on the other hand, we regard scientific knowledge as shifting and tentative – inherently rooted in the 'here and now' of everyday things and events – Early Years science will appear as a natural component of young children's learning and development. Fortunately, many primary teachers in England tend to take the latter view; Johnston and Hayed's international study (1995: 8) found that English primary teachers were more likely to subscribe to a 'process-based' model than other nationalities: 'This emphasis may, in part, be due to the English teachers' interpretation of the question "What do you think science involves?" as "What do you think school/primary science involves?"' Scientific processes (exploration, observation, asking questions, trying things out) are certainly very important aspects of Early Years science. Indeed, we would argue that the younger the child, the greater the emphasis that needs to be placed on the *procedural* ('doing') aspect, in comparison with the *conceptual* ('understanding') components of scientific learning. Not that we would wish to separate these elements; for young children doing is intimately bound up with knowing, and both depend fundamentally upon the development of scientific *attitudes*. Children's emotional disposition towards learning, and their responses to natural phenomena, can serve as the starting points for developing the attitudes of curiosity, open-mindedness and respect for evidence.

Why design & technology in the Early Years?

D&T is an educational invention; it does not exist outside school settings, though it relates in some ways to the tasks performed by different types of professional designers, technologists and engineers. Although the term was in use before 1988, it was the National Curriculum Design and Technology Working Group who in their visionary *Interim Report* (1988: 2) gave it a robust educational rationale:

> Our use of design and technology as a unitary concept, to be spoken in one breath as it were . . . is intended to emphasise the intimate connection between the two activities as well as to imply a concept which is broader than either design or technology individually and the whole of which we believe is educationally important.

Design & technology – spoken as a singular rather than plural term – is a holistic activity, involving thinking and doing, action and reflection. In this respect it parallels many approaches to Early Years education, including 'High/Scope' (see Chapter 2) with its emphasis upon the 'plan–do–review' cycle to develop intentionality in children's play. We believe that purposeful making – giving new arrangements to materials, textures, colours, shapes – is central to young children's quests to bring pattern and order to their physical environments. From their earliest manipulations of blocks, food or soft toys, children show themselves to be born designers. They learn to talk about what they are doing – Piaget's 'egocentric' commentary – and to empathise with the needs and wants of others (real or imagined!), e.g. 'I'm making a bag for teddy'. The problem for practitioners (as with science) is to unpick their own preconceptions about 'technology' and 'design' so they can begin to recognise the D&T happening under their noses.

Research into primary teachers' beliefs about technology (Jarvis and Rennie 1996) has noted – as in the case of science – the strong influence of a model from the school D&T curriculum. Teachers in the study typically cited modern mechanical and electrical products such as computers, telephones and vehicles as 'examples' of technology, with little mention of 'low-tech' examples such as pencils or cups. Food or textiles rarely featured. Non-specialist primary practitioners may regard 'design' as a mysterious language couched in the jargon of 'form' and 'function' from which the general public is largely excluded (Davies 1996). Designers tend to be viewed as 'trendy', 'creative' people concerned with style rather than substance, adding labels to products that increase their value in the market place. The ability to draw well is assumed, which may further alienate teachers who lack confidence in their own drawing. It is important that we expand these limited conceptions of D&T to embrace the creativity of children's experiences with materials, developing their cognitive, manipulative and affective capabilities. Young children 'think' with their hands; their learning is profoundly kinaesthetic and the abstraction of 'drawing before you make' may be irrelevant to Early Years D&T. We want children to have a rich experience of handling designed artefacts from many cultures, and opportunities to fashion objects of beauty for themselves or others, discussing the decisions they are making as they do so.

Why science and D&T together?

By using the statutory curriculum terms 'science' and 'D&T' in this book, we do not want to imply that 'pre-compulsory education is valued only as preparation for the subjects of the National Curriculum rather than as an end in itself' (Hurst 1997: xv). The Early Years curriculum needs to be learner-centred, rather than subject-centred; subject boundaries are the artificial barriers that adults have placed between areas of learning which, for children, form a continuous whole. Nevertheless, as the educational disciplines of science and D&T are currently constructed, they have certain distinctive qualities and purposes which we believe Early Years practitioners need to be aware of in order to successfully integrate them into their practice.

In previous writing (Howe *et al.* 2001; Davies 1997) we have identified a number of ways in which the relationship between D&T and science in the primary curriculum might be conceptualised. One alternative – perhaps attractive in the context of Early Years education – is that we might view the two areas as *indistinguishable*. This approach has considerable precedence in the primary curriculum; one of the defining features of 'informal' practice in England and Wales during the 1970s and '80s was the use of 'topic work' in which the distinction between subjects was deliberately blurred (Alexander *et al.* 1992). In a topic on 'ourselves', for example, choosing fabrics to keep us warm might draw upon science and D&T as strands of learning within the broader realm of understanding, emotional and social skills being developed. In practice, however, this model can often imply a 'primary science and technology' approach in which science plays the dominant role (Ritchie 1995). Any 'making' activities can be seen as an opportunity for children to 'apply' scientific principles they have learned earlier. This is an approach that in our view can be developmentally inappropriate if it implies a progression *from the abstract to the concrete*, whereas we know from experience and research that young children need to begin with concrete experiences.

As currently represented in the National Curriculum, the differences between science and D&T are more clearly accentuated than their similarities. Indeed, D&T has arguably more in common with art & design than it does with science. This is an example of what Gardner (1994) called a *demarcationist* model, leading to the establishment of two distinct subjects, with only very limited links between them.

This too seems to us an inappropriate approach for the Early Years; by treating science and D&T entirely separately practitioners risk missing out on opportunities for contextualising scientific learning through D&T activities. The development of specific knowledge in particular contexts – so-called 'situated cognition' (McCormick *et al.* 1995) – is central to our understanding of young children's learning, and underpins what Gardner (1994) terms a *materialist* model of the interaction between science and D&T in the primary curriculum. The materialist approach elevates D&T to a leading role in the relationship, encouraging practitioners to 'scaffold' children's development of science concepts through the hands-on, familiar contexts provided by evaluating products and solving design problems during making.

While there are clear educational benefits to be gained by framing the Early Years science and D&T curriculum in this way, we would favour an approach that maintains a more 'even' balance between the two areas, such as that implied by Gardner's *interactionist* model (1994) in which they are regarded as distinct yet mutually supportive: 'When the two sets of ideas are brought together they immediately begin to spark off imaginative approaches because they support and complement one another' (Baynes 1992: 35). However, this model begs the following question: which elements do science and D&T share, and how much of each subject should be left in a discrete form? Do the 'technological' aspects of learning (relating perhaps to structures, tools or energy) overlap, while the 'purer' elements of science and design are distinct from one another? We think not. For young children, while a developing understanding of their surroundings and 'how the world works' transcends any subject boundaries, it is in the *processes* informing this understanding that similarities emerge. For example, children *exploring* fabrics in order to find out about their texture and structure may be said to be operating in a scientific mode, while a similar process of exploration undertaken in order to choose materials for a teddy's coat would involve more designerly thinking. While appreciating the similarities and differences between processes used in science and D&T it is important in an interactionist approach to seek ways in which they can 'feed into' one another. For example, the imaging and modelling skills that children develop during D&T activities (Baynes 1992) can support them in developing scientific models and pictures to help understanding of areas such as simple electrical circuits.

But how do science and D&T differ? One useful way of looking at the differences between them is to consider the *purposes* for which we engage in them as activities. As scientists, young children are seeking to understand the world (and beyond) as it exists. They are trying out new ideas (e.g. 'light objects float') to see how useful they are in explaining the phenomena they observe. The product of scientific enquiry is a body of 'tested' knowledge and understanding for the enquirer. By contrast, when acting as designers or technologists, children are seeking to *change* the world (or elements of it) to serve a particular purpose. For example, they might be trying to make a boat that will sail across the water tray. Testing materials for their suitability may *appear* to be exactly the same as the scientific activity above.

However, the purpose in the child's mind is different, since he or she is now working towards making something that hasn't existed before. The product of D&T activity is therefore a 'thing' – a changed reality that may take many forms and may also include the development of understanding on the part of the designer. Both activities are driven by human wants and needs: in the case of science it is the desire for understanding; whereas for D&T it is some improvement in our physical environment. On most occasions, for both children and adults, the motivations may be somewhat mixed, but it is useful for us as educators to recognise the scientific and D&T strands within human endeavour.

The interactionist approach to primary science and D&T offers Early Years practitioners a powerful pedagogical tool for maximising children's learning. It does not, however, preclude us from usefully employing one of the other models of the relationship at times as appropriate. Furthermore, it relies upon a sophisticated understanding of the nature of science and D&T and how each contributes to children's learning, which Chapter 2 aims to explore.

The contents of other chapters

In Chapter 2, Stephen Ward and I explore some of the theoretical underpinning for the inclusion of science and D&T in Early Years practice. We argue that our approach is based upon an interactionist view of childhood and go on to review some of the recent research into the human brain that sheds light on the ways in which children's scientific and designerly aptitudes might unfold. We explore the implications of cognitivist learning theories for these areas, including the importance of mental imaging and play in the development of science and D&T. Finally we move on to considering appropriate teaching strategies, stressing the significance of a 'theory of mind' and the legacy of significant schools of Early Years education such as Montessori, High/Scope and Reggio Emilia.

In Chapter 3, Karen McInnes and Jill Williams look at the range of opportunities that exist outside the school setting for developing science and D&T. They start with the earliest experiences babies may have in the home which can underpin later development, then go on to analyse other science and D&T-related resources within the home environment. They provide detailed guidance and case studies illustrating ways in which practitioners in Reception and Nursery settings can capitalise on children's outside experiences, providing a sense of continuity and greater relevance to the science and D&T undertaken in school.

Chapter 4 switches the emphasis towards narrative; an essential feature in the education of young children and a mode of verbal interaction that is also fundamental to science and D&T. Pat Black and Sue Hughes explore the fundamental role of narrative in human culture, including the 'explanatory' stories told to communicate scientific understanding and interpret people's needs and wants for technology. They go on to stress the importance of children's personal narratives in making sense of their environment and telling stories about what they have designed and made. The role of caregiver's narratives in helping children bridge the gap between home and school is also explored through several case studies.

In Chapter 5 Alan Howe and Kendra McMahon make the case for assessment as an integral part of Early Years practice in science and D&T. They describe a number of techniques, including observation, floorbooks, cognitive mapping and concept cartoons, for gaining access to children's scientific and technological ideas. The next part of the chapter focuses on the content of our assessments at both Foundation Stage and Key Stage 1, including suggestions for supporting children's self-assessment of skills, knowledge and attitudes in science and D&T. Chapter 5 concludes with a consideration of the issues surrounding recording progress and reporting to parents.

In Chapter 6 Alan Howe dissects the *Curriculum Guidance for the Foundation Stage* (QCA/DfEE 2000), considering the contribution of science and D&T to the key areas of young children's learning outlined in this document. Through case studies drawn from Reception classes he makes the case for science and D&T to be seen as relevant to personal, social and emotional development; communication, language and literacy; mathematical, physical and creative development, as well as their acknowledged place in children's knowledge and understanding of the world.

Chapter 7 provides practical guidance for Early Years practitioners seeking to plan for science and D&T in the Nursery or Reception class. Tonie Scott and Sandy Sheppard draw upon their own practice to provide models of long-, medium- and short-term planning which make explicit the scientific, designerly and technological skills that children can develop through a range of activities both inside and outside the classroom. They focus on effective planning for adult intervention, including the role of additional adults in the setting, and upon making effective links between home and school.

In Chapter 8 I explore the background knowledge necessary to intervene effectively in children's science and D&T learning. The chapter is split into sections devoted to developing practitioners' own attitudes, skills and concepts in both science and D&T. It contains many specific examples in tables of techniques for working with materials; information about mechanisms and knowledge required to plan the 'next step' in response to children's scientific ideas.

Chapter 9 turns the focus of the book explicitly towards science, with consideration of the types of activities practitioners can provide for children at different levels of structure and guidance and techniques for intervening in exploratory play to elicit and begin to restructure their understanding. I draw examples from the water tray, D&T activities and narrative-initiated activities to suggest ways of questioning children and supporting their development of scientific skills and attitudes.

In the last chapter, Alan Howe and I provide a vision of how children's early designing and making experiences can be developed progressively into Key Stage 1. We consider the nature of progression in D&T in some detail, suggesting starting points and specific support that teachers can offer in order to help children develop their motor skills, procedural and conceptual understanding. We relate this specifi-

cally to the structure provided by the National Curriculum and consider the importance of including all children in an entitlement to high quality educational experience.

Summary

In this chapter I have defined our terms; we see the Early Years as a distinct phase
of education for children between the ages of 3 and 7 (the Foundation Stage and
Key Stage 1 of the National Curriculum in England), though we regard an 'Early
Years approach' as relevant for children outside this age range. I have also indicated
the nature of learning in science and D&T for young children, indicated how practitioners might go about identifying this learning and provided a rationale for an
interactionist approach to these areas of the Early Years curriculum. Finally, I have
outlined the ways in which this approach is underpinned theoretically and supported practically in the other chapters of this book.

CHAPTER 2

Young children as scientists, designers and technologists

Dan Davies and Stephen Ward

Purpose of this chapter

Through reading this chapter you will gain an understanding of

- an interactionist view of childhood and learning
- how various theories of learning and development help us to understand young children as scientists, designers and technologists
- some appropriate Early Years teaching strategies derived from this theoretical background.

Introduction

There are many helpful summaries of research into young children's learning and its implications for Early Years practice: for example Bruce (1997) provides a useful account. It is not our purpose here to add to this body of literature; what we are interested in is how these findings illuminate our understanding of young children as designers and scientists. In this chapter we will refer to a number of significant names, theories and studies in order to extract the messages they have for children's development of specific 'designerly', technological or scientific capabilities. To what extent are the skills and thought processes involved in science and D&T 'natural' to young children? How can we begin to recognise them and create the conditions that allow them to flourish? We suggest tentative answers to these questions, beginning, as always, with the child.

Views of early childhood

Bruce (1997) suggests that three main views of childhood have informed educational thought in the past century:

- *empiricism* – a 'deficit model' of childhood, emphasising the gaps in their knowledge and skill which teachers need to 'fill'

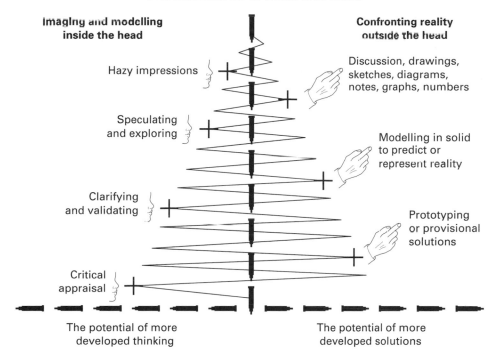

Figure 2.1: A model of a designing process
Source: Kimbell *et al.* (1991)

- *nativism* – that children's development is biologically pre-programmed and there is little educators can do – except to hinder it!
- *interactionism* – that children develop through interactions between their own mental structures, the environment and others.

Interactionism offers in our view the keenest insights into children as scientists and designers. Harlen (2000) offers a model of scientific learning in which the child brings a range of prior experience and ideas into the attempt to make sense of a new phenomenon and works with others to share the ideas they have selected as being most relevant to the situation. Harlen gives the example of a child who, faced with an unfamiliar situation such as two wet wooden blocks sticking together, might suggest they are 'magnets sticking together – perhaps these blocks are magnetic'. This might be where the process ends, unless the presence of another interaction – with a skilled adult who produces a magnet and suggests 'try this' – moves the child forward in the understanding of magnets and forces, to find that 'not everything that sticks together is magnetic'.

In D&T, Kimbell *et al.* (1991) propose a model of designing – 'the interaction of mind and hand' (Figure 2.1) – in which there is an internal dialogue within a child who is struggling to make hazy impressions more concrete by drawing, talking or manipulating materials. The child may be using the wooden blocks to make a boat that got wet by being tested in the water tray. The scientific and D&T elements of learning are interacting as part of the larger interaction between the child's hands, mind, environment and other people. We are therefore interactionist in both our *epistemology* (what we think about knowledge in science and D&T) and our *ontology* (what we think about children and their learning)!

We must not, however, completely ignore what the other two views of childhood may have to tell us about children as scientists and designers. In the nativist tradition, research into the functioning of the human brain may shed light on the mental activity involved in scientific exploration or designing. Fascinating insights have been revealed by recent studies of genetics into the development of the human brain over millions of years to distinguish us so markedly from other primates. However, an interesting finding which emerges from the work of geneticists in the Human Genome Project is how slowly this genetic development has actually occurred. It seems that the hunter-gatherers who survived by roaming the plains 150,000 years ago were at the same stage of genetic development as the baby born yesterday! If we can imagine the baby of a hunter-gatherer being projected forward to be brought up in the twenty-first century, she could just as easily grow up to be a successful microbiologist (Ridley 1999)! What we learn from this is that in all our children we are dealing with potentially great scientists, technologists and designers. Culturally, we stand on the shoulders of those who have gone before us in what we know, but all have the genetic ability to take forward what has gone before.

Young children's brains

Theories of learning that place emphasis upon connections in our brains are given the general term *connectionist theories* (Hill 1997). In their simplest forms, such theories see learning as merely connections between stimuli (what goes in through our senses) and responses (what comes out in our behaviour). This has been used in the past to justify educational practices such as rote learning and teaching through transmission and testing of subject content, clearly deriving from an *empiricist* ('deficit') model of childhood (see above). Some teaching of science, particularly at upper primary level, is still based on this model. However, recent studies of the brain (e.g. Greenfield 2000) and of the ways that computers appear to 'think' and solve problems ('artificial intelligence') have led to more sophisticated 'network' models of learning (Gardner 1999). In such models the brain behaves like a 'wet' computer, forging links between neurons to increase the number of pathways along which electrical signals can travel – our 'parallel processing' capacity. The fundamental importance of these connections in young children's learning is emphasised by Susan Greenfield:

> Although we are born with almost all the neurons we will ever have – some 100 billion – a great many of the connections between these neurons are forged after birth. The growth of new dendrites reaches a peak when we are about 8 months

old, and the process continues apace as we grow. So great is this growth of connections, particularly in the cortex, that the brain has quadrupled in size by the
time we reach adulthood, despite the number of neurons staying roughly the
same.

(Greenfield 2000: 55)

When we think, patterns of electrical activity move in complex ways around our
cerebral cortex, using the connections we have previously made through learning.
This has clear relevance for children as designers and scientists, since it is the ability
to make links between apparently unrelated ideas (e.g. clockwork and radio, the
motion of the planets and a falling apple) that lies at the heart of both creativity and
understanding (Howe *et al.* 2001). As children explore materials and physical or
biological phenomena, physical changes are actually occurring in their brains! The
more of the right kinds of experience they have, the more complex their neural networks will become, but conversely these connections can decay or atrophy through
lack of stimulation – 'use it or lose it'! Not all neural connections necessarily need
interaction in order to develop. For example, Noam Chomsky's (1968) research into
children's language acquisition suggests that the mental structures associated with
speech unfold naturally in a prescribed manner (a *nativist* view – see above). Recent
biological studies have shown the importance of 'sensitive' or 'critical' periods in
human development (Bateson and Martin 2000). A well-known example of the
critical period for learning is in the development of language. A child exposed to
adult language is guaranteed to learn it up to the age of six. After that time the sub-
tleties of a language, such as accent and intonation, become more difficult to learn.
The effect can be demonstrated in those who learn a second or foreign language later
in life. Once language is learned there is no need for the neural circuitry of language
acquisition, and, like a scaffolding around a new building, it is dismantled. So different parts of the brain have to be used to learn a foreign language from the parts used
to acquire the child's first language. But why should the brain close down these circuits to prevent further learning in this way? Pinker (1994: 289) gives a biological
explanation for why the brain benefits from this apparently destructive process:
'Metabolically, the brain is a pig. It consumes a fifth of the body's oxygen and similarly large proportions of calories and phospholipids. Greedy neural tissue lying
around beyond its point of usefulness is a good candidate for the recycling bin.' So
it seems that human beings are neurally programmed to acquire certain skills and
knowledge from their environment in ways which are benefical to them, and one
feature of the theory of critical periods for development is the notion of comple-
tion. The analogy used by some writers is that of a window which opens and then
closes, suggesting that when the critical period is over the learning will be
'imprinted' or fixed and cannot be changed. The example of language acquisition,
as we have shown, illustrates this. Another obvious example is the way people learn
to like certain foods which they are brought up on and find new tastes impossible
to cope with. However, more recent evidence from biological studies reveals that the

window can be kept open: 'the evidence from real organisms reveals a dynamic interplay between the individual's internal organisation and the external conditions. The actual chemistry of sensitive periods does not look at all like a computer program' (Bateson and Martin 2000: 162). So the theory of critical periods underlines the importance of ensuring that young learners are inducted into the methods of thinking required of scientific and designerly thinking and that windows to learning are kept open. Could it be that parts of the brain associated with scientific or designerly thought processes are also to an extent genetically pre-programmed?

Are there parts of the brain associated with science and D&T?

Howard Gardner (1983) identified seven (later nine) distinct 'intelligences' that he claims are associated with specific areas of the brain and are developed to a greater or lesser extent in every individual. In his original model there are linguistic, logical-mathematical, spatial, musical, bodily-kinaesthetic, intrapersonal and interpersonal intelligences. You will have noticed that science and D&T do not feature in the above list, yet it could be argued that elements of all of Gardner's multiple intelligences contribute to both areas (see Alan Howe's discussion of the Curriculum Framework for the Early Years in Chapter 6). The closest parallels in our view can be made with spatial intelligence:

> Central to spatial intelligence are the capacities to perceive the visual world accurately, to perform transformations and modifications upon one's initial perceptions, and to be able to re-create aspects of one's visual experience, even in the absence of relevant physical stimuli.
>
> (Gardner 1983: 173)

Children need spatial intelligence in order to make sense of their observations (of, for example, a battery lighting a bulb when connected by wires) and to construct mental models to explain them (of, say, electricity flowing around in a circuit). Spatial thought also comes into play when they are envisaging how a situation could be different, or how they could use a new discovery in a different context (e.g. picturing the bulb in a lighthouse). The ability to transform or rotate objects in the 'mind's eye' is crucial to the work of scientists and designers, but so is a systematic approach to tackling problems. This is where Gardner's logical-mathematical intelligence comes in: 'This form of thought can be traced to a confrontation with the world of objects . . . the roots of the highest regions of logical, mathematical and scientific thought can be found in the simple actions of young children upon the physical objects in their worlds' (Gardner 1983: 128–9). This is our argument in a nutshell; every time children pick up, squash, slide or roll objects, arrange them in lines or build them into towers, they are exercising those parts of their brains concerned with logical-mathematical thought; they are *being* scientists and designers. Some may be better at it than others (aspects of our brains concerned with space and logic may be 'pre-programmed' to an extent) but the incredible plasticity of young children's nervous systems means that all can improve. The role of 'emotional encoding' (Gardner 1999) here is crucial; children need to feel good about themselves in order to learn, and the emotions are just as fundamental to the functioning of the brain as is 'logical' thought. Scientists and designers both work through their emotions; a scientific theory or design solution must 'feel right', and the emotional energy needed to overcome setbacks is sometimes immense. As educators, we need to support children through their frustrations when things 'won't go right' and not let them reach complete exasperation, which might inhibit the growth of neural connections we are seeking. But can brain studies really give us the whole story? For more guidance on the types of experiences and interventions needed to develop science and D&T we need to look to psychological understandings of children's development and the theories of instruction that have come from them.

Theories of child development

It was the Swiss psychologist Jean Piaget (1929) who first drew attention to the developmental aspects of learning, pointing out that cognitive development occurs in a sequence of phases. For example, he described children's early cognitive attributes as 'egocentric'; by this he meant that the child can only perceive the world in relation to herself. An example Piaget gives is of the child walking along at night who perceives the moon to be moving with her as she walks. Indeed, the moon does appear to do this, but the more mature intellect can reason that the moon must be independent of her own movement, leading to the conclusion that the appearance is a false one. Another effect of 'egocentricity' which Piaget describes is the tendency which young children have of talking to themselves as they engage in actions; so a child arranging cars in a row will say, 'This one goes here, and then another blue one and now a red one.' This communication with the self is what the Russian psychologist Vygotsky (1962) describes as self-directed thought; he sees it as an essential aspect of cognition. Piaget suggests that around the ages of 4, 5 or 6, this egocentric speech which is not addressed to others dies out and the child learns to engage in what he calls 'socialised speech'. Vygotsky acknowledges what Piaget has seen, that the egocentric speech disappears. However, he goes on to suggest that, while the egocentric speech is not audible to the listener in the older child, it continues in the form of silent, or 'inner', speech. In fact, he goes further to say that egocentric or inner speech actually *is* thought. So Piaget's model of the child talking to herself about her actions becomes, instead, the child guiding her own thoughts through action and ultimately engaging in abstract thought. Vyogtsky's model, then, underlines the importance of action as the essential accompaniment to, and facilitator of, thinking. This model corresponds closely with the interaction of hand and eye in designing, referred to above. Our actions as designers are the outward expression of our inner dialogue about what this new thing will be like. For the young child, both action and speech are external, giving us insights into their designing strategies.

Piaget's mechanisms for cognitive growth and change – *assimilation* and *accommodation* – are particularly relevant to young children's scientific learning. For example, a child with the *schema* (elementary concept) that all birds are ducks may easily assimilate the information that male and female mallards, though they look different, are both ducks. She may, however, need to accommodate (adapt) her schema to the revelation that the large white duck she has seen is in fact a swan. This mechanism has been incorporated into a 'constructivist' teaching sequence (von Glasersfeld 1978; Harlen and Osborne 1985) as the *restructuring* phase, in which an adult supports a child through the process of conceptual change (see 'Teaching' below).

Piaget's is a deficit model of the child as the learner: his developmental stages tend to define what the child *cannot* do. For example, we might expect that an egocentric child will be unable to design for others, since the ability to empathise with another person's needs will be developmentally beyond them. Our experience, however, is that given a meaningful context (such as a story) young children can very well appreciate the three little pigs' need for protection. Piaget's work was put into perspective by Margaret Donaldson (1978), who showed that his experimental approach to investigating children's intellectual development was affected by the context and the type of situations in which they found themselves. She found that where activities were introduced in a way that made sense to children in relation to their previous experience, they were capable of what she called 'disembedded thinking' – a more abstract type of thought that children need in order to grasp scientific concepts and imagine future possibilities: 'The paradoxical fact is that disembedded thinking, although by definition it calls for the ability to stand back from life, yields its greatest riches when it is conjoined by doing' (Donaldson 1978: 83). This points again to the value of hands-on experiences with objects and materials in helping to develop higher-order thinking skills in young children. A positive view of the child is also offered by Jerome Bruner (1963), who describes three ways in which young children represent their experiences: the *enactive,* the *iconic* and the *symbolic.* At the enactive stage in babyhood the child's main form of representation is through actions, grasping things and putting them in the mouth. Later, at the iconic stage, she is affected by the appearance of things (for example, representing the moon as a crescent or the sun with 'rays'). The child ultimately grasps the symbolic systems (including language but also the visual language of design) in order to be able to detach herself from the immediate here-and-now of appearances. Bruner, then, shows us the ways that action, visual images and symbolic thinking are interrelated: a strong interactionist argument for scientific and design experiences for young children. In the Early Years children move between these forms of representation and they are the ways in which we can characterise their learning and actions as we observe them: 'The move from "embedded" to "disembedded" thinking . . . depends on acquiring, first, the ability to develop internal representations of experience, and secondly, a facility for deploying these in such a way as to distance oneself from the context' (Blenkin and Kelly 1988:19). Activities that demand representation – symbolic play, drawing, making – will be of the greatest value in providing this key to abstract thinking, provided that children are able constantly to refer back to the concrete situation. At present in Western culture, our 'conventional' ways of representing experience (books, plays, equations) do not sufficiently emphasise visual or spatial representations (drawings, models, patterns). We need to ensure that in our Early Years settings this imbalance is challenged. This need is emphasised by the work of Kosslyn (1978: 316) into mental imagery and the ways we interpret the pictures in our heads. Children, he argues, are more likely to use pictorial images than adults, since if 'fewer facts are encoded explicitly, or if deduction is difficult, imagery is increasingly likely to be used'. When retrieving or representing these images, Kosslyn found that children were likely to select parts defined first by contour, then colour, then texture. In other words they are particularly sensitive to the outline shape of objects; an important attribute for both observing the world and designing new forms.

The importance of play in young children's science and D&T

Much of what we have described above occurs spontaneously in young learners. Many cognitive psychologists agree that children are active in their exploration of the world and generation of new mental structures. Few Early Years practitioners will need convincing of the crucial role of play in young children's learning. Play, 'when in full-flow, helps us to function in advance of what we can actually do in our real lives' (Bruce 1994: 193). But what kinds of play lend themselves to developing learning in science and D&T? Tina Bruce (1994: 190) cites the example of a young boy throwing sticks at walls, bushes and into water, which she compares with children by the river Nile who have made boats: 'He's playing with forces, crashes, splashes, just as they are when they are throwing sticks and large stones into the Nile around the boats that they have made.' As well as dealing with scientific principles, this kind of play is imaginative, therefore feeding the creation of the mental images discussed above, enabling these children to conceive what they have never experienced in the actual world, and hence to start the process of designing: 'From the beginning, the direct use of the hand, and later of tools and materials, is more than a way of simply carrying ideas into production. It is also a way of having new ideas: it is part of the mental equipment that supports the imagination' (Baynes 1992: 28). Bruner *et al.* (1976) have arrived at significant insights into children's play and its role in enabling them to negotiate, solve problems and imagine alternative futures – all crucial design capabilities. Bruner and his colleagues observed children playing with objects in different structured situations. In one such experiment, children were classified in terms of their attitude to a specially designed toy and the playfulness with which they interacted with it. 'The more inventive and exploratory the children had been initially in playing with the super-toy, the higher their originality scores were four years later' (Bruner *et al.* 1976: 17). Significantly, Bruner's 'play' groups outperformed 'taught' groups consistently. One of the fundamental characteristics of play is that it is low-risk; we cannot be wrong when playing. The security this gives to the player enables her to take risks – the experience gives her confidence to be inventive and make mistakes when the situation becomes more structured. Thus the ability to solve problems is linked closely with the freedom to play. Moyles (1989: 63) identifies 'specific exploration' as being that kind of play which looks at what the material is and what it can do, and 'diversive exploration' as leading a child to explore what *they* can personally do with the material. For example, a child might manipulate playdough for some time, exploring its properties (a scientific type of enquiry), then later start to make an animal out of it (beginning to engage in designing and making). Similarly, Corrinne Hutt's taxonomy of children's play (1979) has close links with scientific and designerly exploration. She distinguishes between play which is *epistemic* (problem-solving, exploratory, concerned with skills) and *ludic* (symbolic, repetitive, fantasy, concerned with innovation). Again, it is tempting to see these as scientific and designerly forms of play respectively, though this may be over-simplistic since science can be imaginative: 'Through epistemic behaviour the child acquires information, knowledge and skills. Ludic behaviour allows children to make the understandings their own' (Riley and Savage 1994:136). One feature of ludic play is its use of *schemas* (see above). These are patterns of 'repeatable behaviour into which experiences are assimilated and that are gradually co-ordinated' (Athey 1990: 37). For example, a child may be fascinated by putting objects into bags or wrapping them up, while repeatedly drawing enclosed circular shapes (an envelopment schema). Schemas have dynamic (moving) and configurative (still) aspects; unsurprisingly perhaps adults tend to encourage the latter! Schemas tend not to be isolated patterns of behaviour – they develop in clusters and are part of whole networks of senses, actions and thinking, characteristic of Piaget's 'sensori-motor' stage of development between the approximate ages of 2 and 4. Schemas are thought to be important stages in the development of key concepts, many of which may have scientific or technological links, as in Table 2.1.

If adults are alert to these schemas and can provide materials that help children to explore them fully, they can help to support this conceptual development. Another feature of ludic (imaginative) play which is of particular value to children's designerly development is the blurring between fantasy and reality in, for example, setting up a model town. The distinction between 'inside' and 'outside' the head is less clear-cut and more easily crossed during play, a situation analogous to the modelling activities of designers:

> In some ways, children are more adept at using models than adults. For infants, the division between model and reality is blurred and all children up to the age of 13 can get thoroughly lost in the world of imagination represented by role-play, fantasy, toys, drawings and models. Many adult designers would give a lot to be able to enter the imagined future in such a wholehearted way.
>
> (Baynes 1992: 20)

Such activities also have a strong emotional content; children learn to empathise with the feelings of the imaginary characters in their play scenarios, enabling them

Table 2.1: Possible connections between children's early schemas and later scientific and technological concepts or activities

Early schema	Later concept/activity
Transporting – a child may move an object or collection from one place to another	Designing vehicles, carriers, conservation of matter
Vertical – actions such as climbing, stepping up or down	Lifts, escalators, cranes, work with construction kits
Intersections – e.g. drawing many criss-crossing lines	Joining materials, e.g. strips of wood
Circular – circles may appear in drawings, paintings and collages	Wheels and axles, electrical circuits
Core and radial – circles with radiating lines, e.g. 'tadpole' figures	Minibeasts in nature, flowers and plants

Source: adapted from Bruce (1997: 79)

to move from an egocentric viewpoint to considering the needs of others in future designing. As they develop, children's play becomes more rule-bound and follows clear procedures as in the playing of games. This too can help with understanding of processes and procedures in scientific enquiry (planning, predicting, interpreting) and D&T (proposing, making, evaluating).

Teaching young children science and D&T

We have looked at children's spontaneous learning, yet there is clearly also a role within an interactionist view for a 'more knowledgeable other' – the teacher or practitioner. Much of Bruner's work on play and child development has been translated into a *theory of instruction* – what we as adults can do to support and enhance learning. The overall structure for this theory is his notion of the *spiral curriculum*, which suggests positively that it is possible for all learners to acquire any type of knowledge at an appropriate level:

> you begin with an 'intuitive' account that is well within the reach of a student, and then circle back to a more formal or highly structured account, until, with however many more recyclings are necessary, the learner has mastered the topic or subject in its full generative power.
>
> (Bruner 1996: 119)

Whitebread (1996: 6) interprets this model in an Early Years context as children encountering a set of ideas at a practical level when they are young, which will help them understand the same ideas at a more symbolic or abstract level later. For example, a child pushing a trolley who notices that it is harder to push when loaded with bricks will have the intuitive basis for understanding Newton's second law of motion (force equals mass times acceleration) some years later. This will be much more likely, however, if a knowledgeable adult has been with them in the early experience, encouraging them to talk about the 'heaviness' (inertia) they feel with the loaded trolley.

This kind of support has been described by Bruner as 'scaffolding' – taught steps to bridge the gap between the child's unaided understanding or capability and that which they have the potential to achieve in the near future. This crucial area of learning what they 'just don't quite know' has been called the 'zone of proximal development' by Lev Vygotsky (1962), who emphasises the vital role of social interaction to support the learner's own efforts within this zone. Within the field of primary science education in particular, the notion of young children 'constructing' their understandings of the world has become popular, deriving from the work of Ernst von Glasersfeld (1989): 'The child must interpret the task and try to construct a solution by using material she already has . . . The teacher's role is to gain understanding of the child's understandings' (von Glasersfeld 1989: 14). In order to help children as learners we need to interpret their actions and, thereby, to understand their thinking. Bruner (1996) points out that one of the features which differentiates human beings from other primates is that human beings 'teach' their young. Other creatures learn in various ways and some – chimpanzees for example – can be seen to be quite sophisticated learners. However, although young chimpanzees learn, often through imitation, adult chimpanzees do not actually teach. Bruner explains that, in order to teach, we need a 'concept of mind'; we need to be able to assess what it is that the child knows, doesn't know or needs to know. It is only human beings that have this ability to see into the mind of others and it enables us to make judgements about how to structure our behaviour to aid the learner. In its simplest form this might be to demonstrate, or model, the actions that we want the child to be able to repeat. So we might demonstrate how to make marks on a board with chalk and the child, or indeed a chimpanzee, might pick up the chalk and imitate the action. The difference between the adult human and the adult ape, however, is that the human intends the child to learn, and the adult's actions may be a kind of 'performance' to be imitated, whereas the ape is simply engaging in self-serving behaviour which is imitated by the young. In the intention to teach is the idea that there is a state of knowledge or skill we want the child to attain and so we adjust our behaviour and engage in actions which will support the learner. It is in order to be able to do this that we need a concept of mind, a way of understanding what the learner needs. Inherent in the concept of mind is another feature of human knowledge known as 'metacognition'. The idea of metacognition is to have cognition (knowledge and skills) but also to *know* what knowledge and skills we have, or are yet to acquire. Metacognition is essential to the business of teaching, as we need to know what we know in order to be able to teach others. Having a concept of mind means that we can guess what others are thinking and what they know. Of course, we may be wrong in what we guess, but the point is that human beings *do* it and good teachers do it *well*. In the example of the child with a trolley above, it would take an experienced practitioner to recognise the concept of inertia being explored intuitively, and to make it more explicit through discussion.

A limited form of teaching is simply to tell, or to demonstrate, what the learner needs to know or do. We shouldn't be too critical of this, since it is based upon decisions about what the learner knows or needs to know, a selection of possible knowledge and a carefully chosen sequence of that knowledge. For example, we might introduce children to the idea of a complete circuit before thinking about breaking that circuit with a switch. These sorts of decisions are based on knowing the material, knowing what are prerequisites and so what needs to come first in an explanation or demonstration. It is likely that the teacher bases the decisions about what and how to teach on what she has learned and how she has learned it, reflecting on her own experience and making assumptions that her learners will learn in a similar way. We should also remember that, in order to learn from this type of teaching, the learner needs to be mentally active; there is no such thing as 'passive learning', and in such a situation it might be said that the learner needs to be especially active.

While such a procedure is a genuine teaching and learning enterprise, the idea of a concept of mind invites us to develop a more sophisticated view of what the learner's mind is and how learners' minds differ. For us to be better teachers it requires that we have the best possible understanding of the psychological learning processes in the child's mind and that we have a sophisticated understanding of the nature of the knowledge we want them to learn. So we need to investigate the latest thinking and research on children's learning (as presented in this chapter) and have clear insights into what scientific and D&T knowledge, processes and attitudes are all about (as introduced in Chapter 1). Not only does the teacher need to have a concept of the learner's mind, but children also need a concept of their own minds (Novak and Gowin 1984). This metacognitive dimension to children's learning means that they can take an evaluative position on their knowledge and skills and the learning processes; for example, 'I like doing science because I can understand the way things work,' or 'I like D&T because I can make really good things.' Such children will not passively accept what the teacher asserts to be worth knowing; instead, it is inherent in learning that they actively make decisions about what is good and worthwhile.

As we have suggested, good teaching and learning requires a good knowledge of the learner's mind; teachers can use different strategies to gain such an understanding. One of these is to 'elicit' the child's current knowledge and understanding (Ollerenshaw and Ritchie 1997) by asking questions, observing them or inviting them to record their ideas in some way. However, there are interesting twists in this process, since another aspect of the child's concept of mind is that she can also have a concept of the teacher's mind; she can have an idea of what the teacher is thinking and know the kinds of things which teachers want. So children soon learn the kind of answers teachers are looking for when they ask questions, and it is possible for children to learn to give the types of replies to questions that they think they are looking for. These might not be the answers which reveal the learner's actual knowledge; for example a child may say that we need a circuit to make a bulb light, while believing one of the wires to be redundant because all the electricity flows down the other! So, ironically, the mutuality of the concept of mind between teacher and learner can actually obstruct the learning process.

A further beneficial aspect of this concept of mind is that learners can have an understanding of each other's minds in a pair or group learning situation. So children are able to negotiate each other's concepts, part of what has been called a 'social constructivist' model of learning. This makes discussions in groups where children initially hold different ideas more productive than those in 'same idea' groups, where they may tend to reinforce rather than challenge misconceptions. So we need to be able to help children in understanding each other's minds as this is central to the notion of 'interactionist' learning. Piaget saw children as needing to *learn* to interact with others as they develop socialised speech. This view has had a profound impact on the thinking of teachers, yet recent research indicates that the interactionist principle is so deeply grounded in human psychology that even babies are interacting meaningfully with others (Trevarthen 1995: 2):

> By about 6 weeks most infants are very alert to the presence of anyone seeking a chat. They look at the person's face, focussing on the eyes, attending to their speech and friendly expressions, and then the baby smiles and begins to make a contribution. The way this early interest in getting into an exchange evolves from moment to moment is most instructive. Both adult and infant act like conversational experts. Both are making bids for the other's interest. Both are pausing to see how the other responds. After a few tentative friendly tries, a real conversational exchange of utterances takes place, the two smoothly turn-taking and co-operating in carrying the pleasure and interest forward.

So the idea here is not that children *learn to be* social, but that they are inherently social and that learning through interaction with others and the understanding of the minds of others is a primary function, not a sophisticated and learned one. Bruner (1996) calls this 'cultural learning' and points to it as a natural consequence of a concept of mind; it is also an essential prerequisite for scientific and designerly learning. So why do we not always find young children ready to interact with others? Pollard and Filer (1999) track the experiences of a group of children through the primary school as they move from class to class and provide fascinating accounts of children's different approaches to the social context of the Reception classroom. While Sarah and Willliam settle confidently into the co-operative group activities, Robert is a child who has achieved a high level of learning at home and finds the presence of others in the classroom a source of frustration:

Robert's plans for achieving the ideas in his head were frequently frustrated . . . other children would often take and use the pieces of equipment that Robert had in mind and he was therefore more likely to see them as a source of frustration in the classroom than as useful co-operators in play.

(Pollard and Filer 1999: 172)

As the year goes on Robert does learn to co-operate and make a success of the social context of the classroom, but his case shows that we need to ensure that children understand the rules of classroom interactions, and even that some children may be successful learning 'loners'.

Models of Early Years practice and the place of science and D&T

Much of the research and many of the principles of young children's learning out-lined in this chapter are present in models of Early Years schooling derived from the work of three educational pioneers: Friedrich Froebel (1782–1852), Maria Montessori (1869–1952) and Rudolf Steiner (1861–1925).

Arguably, each of these models of education are based on an interactionist per-spective. Froebel's view of development is that of the law of opposites. The wooden ball contrasts with the soft ball. New experiences challenge old ones. In this way, maturation and experience constantly interact with each other (Bruce 1997: 33). For Montessori there is a three-way interaction between maturational processes in the child, experiences the child has and the environment he or she is in. Steiner stresses the way that the spirit and body increasingly interact until they fuse. All three approaches place great emphasis upon direct, hands-on experience, together with children taking on responsibility for planning and implementing changes that will enhance their lives and those of others. Scientific and designerly activity as we understand it is central to this approach, and a view that sees these as two facets of the same process, constantly interacting, will be more in tune with the holistic approach to children's learning so valued by each.

In Reggio Emilia, a city in Northern Italy, a model of early childhood education has developed which has attracted worldwide attention and admiration. Running through the practice of a network of pre-schools and infant–toddler centres in the city, serving the needs of children from 3 months to 6 years of age, is the concept of a 'rich' child: 'a child rich in potential and competence and closely connected to the adults and children around. The child is seen as autonomously capable of making meaning from experience, and it is the adult's role to activate this in the child' (Mortimer 2001: 27). This leads to practice in which activities are built around individual children's interests, focusing on art and creative expression, including the types of modelling activities we might recognise as design & technol-ogy. A fifth approach to nursery education – the High/Scope model deriving from the United States – also has what we would understand as a design process at its heart: 'Each child plans their activities for the session or the day in a small group with an adult educator. They then move off to carry out the planned activities, and later return to review progress again with their small group and the adult educator' (Whitebread 1996: 18). The sequence of plan–do–review, so central to the notion of successful scientific enquiry and D&T activity, is therefore enshrined in the centre of one of the most influential models of nursery practice. It may be no exaggeration to say that science and D&T are *central* to high quality Early Years provision.

Summary

In this chapter we have reviewed some of the psychological theory – both connectionist and cognitive – that underpins our model of young children as scientists and technologists. We have seen how theories of brain development support a role for these kinds of learning in the curriculum, and how models of young children's cognitive development have emphasised the role of play in the development of designing skills and led to social constructivist approaches to scientific instruction. Finally, we have looked briefly at some contemporary models of Early Years education and found in them much that is science or D&T-related. Our next task will be to apply these understandings to the contexts in which young children learn.

CHAPTER 3

Science and D&T beyond the classroom

Karen McInnes and Jill Williams

Purpose of this chapter

Through reading this chapter you will gain an understanding of

- children's varying everyday scientific and technological experiences and the knowledge that they bring to school with them
- ways in which these experiences and knowledge should form a foundation for learning in the classroom
- strategies for building genuine communication between home and school.

Introduction

Chapter 2 has established our interactionist approach to science and D&T education. This approach is most effective when there is recognition of its significance to the development of even the youngest children in their home environments and the experiences that they later bring with them to the school situation. This chapter considers how teachers can recognise this experience and the knowledge, skills and understanding which young children are gaining in the environment beyond the school. It also considers how teachers can improve the science and D&T learning experiences that they are providing in school to build upon this rich, holistic knowledge. Home and school are, of course, not the only settings in which such learning takes place. As emphasised in the introductory chapter, this discussion is relevant to practitioners working in playgroups and day nurseries as well.

Science and D&T from birth

Chapter 2 has already provided a theoretical underpinning for young children's learning in science and D&T. For the purposes of this chapter, it is worth emphasising that these processes begin long before children enter school. Babies are born to learn (Karmiloff-Smith 1994). They enter the world with their senses attuned to make sense of their surroundings. They can distinguish the smell of their mother's milk within hours of being born. They can recognise sounds they have heard many times while in the womb, and within just three to four days they recognise their mother's voice. They continue to use their senses to build up a mental picture of the world which becomes progressively more complex. This is an active process. Babies do not just respond to stimuli but also initiate interactions and in doing so show an ability to motivate and control people around them. Smiling at adults, which can occur from three to four weeks of age, elicits non-verbal and verbal reactions from people around her, which provide the baby with further stimuli from which to learn.

As well as initiating responses, babies are active in another way – they move a lot. Initially, movements comprise a set of reflexes that are unintentional and jerky. However, quite quickly movements become more refined and intentional and enable the baby to explore and learn more about the world. There is evidence that through movement babies develop fresh neural connections in the brain; moving is thinking to a newly born infant. There are echoes in this of the interaction between mind and hand in D&T (see Figure 2.1). To be most productive in learning, however, a baby needs responsive and supportive adults who will provide feedback to her actions, expressions and utterances.

As babies become toddlers and young children, their learning processes come increasingly to resemble those we associate with scientific enquiry: 'They formulate theories, make and test predictions, seek explanations, do experiments and revise what they know in the light of new evidence. These abilities are at the core of the success of science' (Gopnik *et al.* 1999: 161). One developmental example of this is the rooting reflex whereby a baby's head will turn towards the cheek or side of the mouth being touched. This quickly develops into mouthing whereby all objects are put to the mouth to be explored (Bruce and Meggitt 1996). In putting objects into their mouths babies are using all their senses to investigate the objects. On the basis of the touch of the object they will form theories about how the object will taste or smell. They then test these theories out. In doing this babies are constantly engaging in mini-investigations with objects.

An example is Karen's daughter Sophie at the age of two months. While being changed she would lie on her changing mat with a multi-gym placed over her in her line of vision and within her reach. She would constantly attempt to hit the objects dangling in front of her face. In doing this she was engaging in scientific exploration, formulating hypotheses concerned with distance, her own reach and the likely effects of her actions on the swaying motion of the toys. Finally, she achieved her goal of hitting one of the objects, proceeding to engage in further experimentation as she started hitting all the objects with varying degrees of force. Achieving her desired goal also meant that she was displaying an important scientific attitude, that of persistence. Babies and young children can spend surprisingly long periods of time engaged in such exploratory behaviour (Roden 1999). This repetitive behaviour was motivated by the satisfying colours, shapes and movement of the multi-gym, so it also demonstrates Sophie's emerging design awareness. Coordinating perception and action to make contact with objects in the outside world is an early stage in the development of tool use (Karmiloff-Smith 1994), so the experience could also be said to prefigure her development as a tool user and ultimately a designer.

So, if babies and young children are naturally engaged in learning as young scientists, designers and technologists, in what ways can the home environment support such learning?

The home as a science and D&T learning environment

The home provides a powerful learning context for very young children (Tizard and Hughes 1984; Fisher 1996; Parkinson and Thomas 1999). Learning in the home is necessarily holistic and cross-curricular, but it is the *interactive processes* by which home learning comes about that make it such a supportive learning environment for budding scientists and designers: 'Simply by being around their mothers, talking, arguing and endlessly asking questions, the children were being provided with large amounts of information' (Tizard and Hughes 1984: 251). According to Tizard and Hughes, there are four important factors that make the home an effective learning environment. All four factors are true of both parental and childminder's homes; all have relevance to learning in science and D&T.

- The first factor is the wide range of activities that can occur in the home, many of which have a scientific or D&T content. For example, cooking, gardening, washing the dishes, caring for a baby or pet, trips to the park, all involve some degree of planning, re-arrangement or change in materials and empathy for the needs of others.
- The second factor is the shared experience and sustained interactions between adult and child, which enable the adult to understand and make sense of the child's emerging understanding of the world. This also provides for continuity and progression of learning in the home as both adult and child have a shared knowledge of prior learning, which can be built upon. Coupled with this is the low adult-to-child ratio found in most homes. This provides more opportunities for in-depth conversations and question-asking – an important part of scientific learning in particular.
- Thirdly, learning in the home is embedded in contexts that are meaningful to the child. For example, talking to a child about the changes that are happening as you melt butter to make a cheese sauce for dinner can be more meaningful than a more abstract discussion in a classroom context. We recently observed a class of Reception children watching a chocolate bar being melted in a microwave oven. Unable to touch and barely able to see, the children were learning that chocolate melts when microwaved. Of course, it could have been done with a visible source of heat but this may be more difficult to organise safely in the classroom than in a home environment.

- The final and perhaps most important factor mentioned by Tizard and Hughes as advantaging the home as a learning environment is the close relationship between the adult and the child. This enables anxieties and concerns to be expressed so that natural curiosity can be supported and a deeper level of learning can be achieved. Although the emotional bond may not be as strong, this factor can also be significant in the homes of childminders. Childminders often care for the same children from a young age and develop close relationships with them. They understand the children in their care, ask them questions and support their learning in meaningful ways. They have many of the same kinds of resources and undertake many of the same kinds of activities that children would experience in the parental home. In addition, they have often received training in childcare and educational provision, may be better equipped for resourcing 'messy' activities and may have more time for direct interaction with children than busy parents.

So, given these natural advantages, what are the types of resources and activities in the home environment that provide opportunities for learning in science and design & technology?

Resources in the home environment for science and D&T

There is a wealth of different types of science and D&T-related toys, games and resources available to parents and childminders, ranging from traditional wooden bricks to computer games. Such resources can allow children to explore a wider range of materials and phenomena at home than in times gone by (Cohen 2002). However, as we have already emphasised, it is often the everyday activities and the resources used to accompany them that provide the greatest potential to stimulate young children's scientific exploration and designerly creativity.

For very young babies Goldschmied and Jackson (1994) suggest assembling a 'treasure basket' to provide a powerful and multi-sensory learning resource. This approach is most appropriate for babies who can sit up but are not yet mobile. It consists of a basket filled with a variety of natural, everyday resources that can be found in the home which stimulate the different senses: for example, a lemon for taste, smell and vision, a metal chain for touch, a bicycle bell for hearing. By playing with the different resources babies are developing manipulative skills and are using all their senses to experiment with and find out about the objects. Important first steps in decision-making are taken as they observe, select and return to favoured objects. The adult's role in this play situation is to observe and support the baby by providing encouraging smiles and words.

For older babies who are mobile, a progression from the treasure basket can be towards heuristic play with objects (Goldschmied and Jackson 1994). Heuristic play involves active exploration of objects found around the home. Tins, woollen pom-poms, small bags and clothes pegs are all examples of the types of resources used by children during this type of play. However, in heuristic play children not only explore the resources but also combine them in different ways, introducing elements of designing and making. In bringing objects together through joining, building and balancing, children are taking developmental steps on the path to becoming a competent designer (QCA/DfEE 2000). Again, the adult's role involves encouraging and supporting the child's play without necessarily intervening.

Treasure baskets and heuristic play enable babies and very young children to act as scientists and designers in the home. For older children an everyday activity such as cooking provides opportunities for an informal lesson in food technology. When two-year-old Millie and seven-year-old Sophie helped make a mushroom pie for dinner they engaged in scientific and technological behaviour at different developmental levels. They used different tools for different purposes. Sophie used a knife to chop onions and mushrooms into small pieces. Millie used a whisk to beat eggs and cream and mix them together. They both rolled pastry with varying degrees of success owing to the different weights of rolling pin that they were able to handle. They used a variety of cutters to design and make patterns with pastry for the lid of the pie; they observed and asked questions as they watched the changes that occur in onions and mushrooms as they cook. They used scientific language ('soft', 'sticky', 'crumbly') to describe the feeling of rubbing the fat into the flour to make crumbs and then adding the water to make the pastry dough. The purpose behind this activity – preparing the evening meal – embedded these skills and processes in a meaningful context.

Although parents may not explicitly plan for such experiences, childminders – now subject to Ofsted inspections – often produce plans to show the play activities which children will engage with while in their care. Ongoing activities such as messy play with playdough, cutters and rollers, glue, paper, glitter and stickers all provide opportunities for using tools and materials creatively. Construction toys such as Duplo, Mega Blocks and Popoids allow children to build assorted constructions and engage in designing and making. Summer play in the sand pit, with water and/or bubbles, allows children to observe, describe and investigate, e.g. 'Would a square bubble-blower give us square bubbles?' Trips to the park and the woods enable children to explore the natural environment, observing and classifying living things at first hand. Some of the childminder's monthly objectives may focus on D&T processes. For example, making box models involves children selecting appropriate shapes and sizes of box, working out ways of joining them together to achieve a desired effect and using finishing techniques such as painting, colouring or applying other materials. While engaged in these activities children will be asking questions and talking about the activity, while the childminder scaffolds their developing understandings through discussion and suggestions, e.g. 'Have you tried . . . ?'

Bridging the gap between home and school

Early Years practitioners recognise the need to take into account the experiences that children bring to school with them and to 'build on what children already know and can do' (QCA/DfEE 2000: 11). How can we avoid paying lip-service to this request and become sensitive to the attitudes and skills that have already formed a basis for children's learning? The varied knowledge of the world that children have gained is implicit and embedded in their continuing home experience. It may be dependent on the original context and seem tenuous in the unfamiliar classroom situation. The knowledge may appear to be irrelevant to the child when new demands seem to discount previous understanding, and it may well be ephemeral if not tapped into and integrated into the school curriculum. The research by Tizard and Hughes (1984) and Wells (1986) demonstrated how little knowledge teachers had of the lives led by the children in their care.

For example, Jill's son Tom was four-years-old when he announced that his snowman had started to *disappear*. They brought a part of the snowman inside and watched it slip into a pool of water. They melted and re-froze ice cubes, warmed butter and lit candles. Tom picked at spilt wax that had solidified on the kitchen table and tried to reconstitute the melted butter by whisking it furiously. He seemed happy with his exploration at that point. About a month later, when he was watching his grandfather put sugar into his tea, he said, 'Is the sugar melting?' This led to discussion of dissolving and observation that there was sugar at the bottom of the cup. He discovered that there was a residue when there was too much sugar in the tea and none when there was only one spoonful. The next day we made a jelly to reinforce his interest and talked about the relationship between the change in temperature and change of state. As a spin-off from these brief encounters, Tom spent the next week freezing water in any containers he could find and using the ice shapes as a fantasy world for his model dinosaur collection! In the home the child may well have more chance to explore, hypothesise, have questions answered and have opportunities to further his understanding than in the school situation. It is not surprising therefore that some years later Tom returned from school one day and asked, 'Why am I allowed to use clay at home and put it away by myself when in school I am told that I can't use it because there is no one to supervise me?'

Another issue in making effective links between home and school learning is that of holism (see Chapter 1). The *Curriculum Guidance for the Foundation Stage* (QCA/DfEE 2000) groups the subjects children will come to know as science and D&T under the umbrella of Knowledge and Understanding of the World, one of six such headings. Children at home learn from everything that happens to them and do not separate their experiences into subjects (Siraj-Blatchford and MacLeod-Brudenell 1999). Alan Howe in Chapter 6 argues that science and D&T actually contribute to all six areas of the Foundation Stage curriculum, yet we could equally well suggest that Knowledge and Understanding of the World should embrace the whole curriculum and include the creative, physical, mathematical, linguistic and personal and social aspects of learning. Integration of areas of learning is important if we are to appreciate the relevance that scientific and technological ideas have for young children's holistic experience of their world, both at home and at school.

We recognise that in recent years there has been a very welcome, renewed focus on the education and care of young children. Unfortunately, however, recent strategies and guidelines have limited teachers' abilities to broaden possibilities for learning. Time for honest discussion between children and adults is often not valued in school settings. There is also a fear that by responding to children's spontaneous ideas or following the interests they bring from home there may be deviation from what has been planned for their learning. For example, in earlier writing I cite the example of Darren, whose overriding passion was the mini car that he was renovating with his father (Williams 2003). He had helped to strip the engine and rebuild the bodywork, yet this experience and his extensive knowledge of the internal combustion engine was not seen to be relevant to his learning experiences in school.

Our conversations with teachers have revealed the tension they feel between giving time to understand what children already know and the time given to ensure that children understand what is being taught. Marion Dowling (2002) expresses concern about the 'hurry along pace' that places children under pressure in their home lives as well as their lives in school. If we allow this pace to destroy our belief in the careful preparation that is necessary for any successful outcome then we are in danger of wasting many precious opportunities for scientific and technological learning.

Of course, we cannot assume that all children are coming to us with the same richness of home learning experience. In the home situation it is not always easy to support children's curiosity effectively (Siraj-Blatchford and MacLeod-Brudenell 1999). There are often time and mood constraints, and parents may also lack the confidence or background knowledge to judge how best to respond to a child's question. Children need to indulge in fantasy and poetic licence at times, and at other times they need a scientific or technological explanation that is suited to their level of understanding (Donaldson 1992). At the opposite extreme, some parents may be too quick to offer an answer which baffles the child or shuts down the discussion. Many Nursery and Reception classes provide induction guides for parents to support their child's learning in the lead-up to starting school. These may suggest strategies such as clarifying the question ('What makes you ask that?' 'What do you mean by . . . ?'), asking the child for his or her own ideas or suggesting, 'Let's find out together' by looking in a book or CD-ROM.

Comparing science and D&T learning at home and at school

We need to consider the similarities and differences between children's opportunities for learning in the home and those in the school. Perhaps then we can find ways of complementing the range of technological and scientific opportunities that children may be having at home with opportunities for extending and developing these experiences within the Early Years curriculum.

Typically, the home can provide

- opportunities for incidental as well as planned learning
- spontaneous, everyday situations that challenge children's thinking by raising genuine problems
- familiar adults and peers who may respond to questions and encourage follow-up experiences
- lack of pressure to arrive at outcomes with a prescribed formula
- play/learning opportunities that are not defined by a timetable and can continue over long periods if necessary
- no need for perfection because there is no pressure from competition and no audience other than close family members
- opportunity for improvisation and innovation because rarely will specific materials have been provided
- no requirement for assessment other than the intuitive, ongoing assessment that takes place when concerned adults monitor children's interests
- high quality verbal interaction that may include recall and reminiscence, concern with the 'here and now' and prediction.

By contrast, the school typically offers

- opportunities to advance children's learning
- experiences that allow specific curriculum outcomes to be achieved
- experiences that may require a uniform 'end product'
- carefully planned experiences
- opportunities for interaction with children that is generally designed to elicit knowledge
- structures for monitoring children and assessing their learning.

The points above provide a general picture of opportunities for learning in home and school and will not reflect the experiences of all children in either situation. Schools do, however, sometimes take the curriculum brief too seriously and plan against learning objectives at the expense of recognising children's understanding and providing tasks that are relevant to them. It is not possible to match the curriculum to the needs of each child, but the opportunities provided should have general relevance to the age and the stage of the children in the group. Similarly they should draw on children's interests and current knowledge. Making positive responses to children's spontaneous discovery, intense interest and questions can lead to learning that has immediate relevance and a chance for ongoing investigation.

How can D&T and science in school link more closely to children's experiences in the wider world?

It is important to start from the premise that there are opportunities for a range of spontaneous starting points as well as planned experiences in school and in the home. The examples presented below show different ways in which teachers have been able to make these links real. They have been drawn from observation and case studies over a period of time, involving children from different social and ethnic backgrounds.

Preparing snacks and cooking meals

Food preparation is a part of daily living. Many children will experience 'home cooking' and take part in 'designing' meals. Others will eat ready-prepared snacks and 'fast food'. When children are encouraged to prepare their food they start to take an interest in its taste, texture and variety as well as the techniques and skills needed. The examples that follow show the value placed on food in three different settings.

The children in one village school made a variety of biscuits, prepared fresh fruit and weighed and packaged dried fruit to sell at break time. Each class took their turn at cooking, preparation and presentation and the 'tuck shop' was a regular part of the school's social and economic programme. It drew upon the range of snacks that parents had provided for break time and the discussions children were having at home about healthy eating. The children undertook surveys of food preference among their peers (research), considered the need for a balanced diet (planning) and discussed the success of their shop (evaluation). They collected suggestions for changes from their customers (evaluation).

A nursery school in an ethnically and culturally mixed inner city area used food activities as one way of celebrating diversity. Food preparation involving children and adults working together had become a part of daily life in the classroom. Parents had helped children to design and make a range of food products including samosas and rice dishes, recipes with plantains and elderflower champagne! Preparing food for celebrations involved staff and parents in shopping together and children being involved with preparation, presentation and eating.

Barbara, a childminder, recognised the varying dietary requirements of the children in her care. She talked to parents and worked with vegetarian recipes to create soups and pasta dishes with which children could help. Chopping, peeling, sieving, processing and adding salt and pepper became commonplace practical adult-initiated activities and provided vocabulary and ideas for children's cooking in the role-play areas. Barbara collected a wide range of kitchen artefacts and allowed children to use them in both a representational and a practical way. The children were encouraged to talk about the food they were eating and to plan meals with Barbara.

Playing in the garden

Not all children have a garden, but most have experience of playing outside and all will have encountered small invertebrates ('minibeasts'), developing a fascination with – and maybe a fear of – slugs, spiders, ladybirds and centipedes. The children in one Reception class were given frequent opportunities to talk about home life. Anna arrived one Monday morning, full of her experiences in her garden: 'I saw bumble bees, lady beetles, tiny ants and flies. Bees sting, you know and ants do if they're big. I ran away.' The teacher listened to Anna's vivid recollections and after registration set out, with the children, on a 'minibeast' safari in the school grounds. The children were given the opportunity to collect, observe and release small creatures, set up a 'refuge for snails' and use the overhead projector to create enlarged imaginary worlds using plastic representations of creatures and a variety of translucent and opaque material. Stories, poems and songs relating to minibeasts were introduced and the children showed renewed interest in digging in a patch of land set aside for the purpose. This spontaneous activity ran alongside and complemented other planned curriculum experiences.

Repairing a bicycle puncture

If the use of bicycles is a part of family life most children will have witnessed aspects of their maintenance. Tim and Jenny were twins who had watched their father taking out the inner tube, locating the puncture using a bowl of water and repairing it using a patch and rubber solution. The nursery teacher asked Tim's and Jenny's parents to bring the bicycle and the tools into school and the twins gave an accurate description of the puncture repair. This prompted bicycles being introduced into the nursery playground (begged, borrowed and stolen from parents) and serious development of a 'maintenance area' for bikes, trucks and all wheeled vehicles. Important links were made between bicycle wheels and the wheels of various construction kits in the classroom, developing an early understanding of simple mechanisms in D&T. For the remainder of the term there was increased interest in construction using a variety of improvised and commercial materials. Dramatic play increased with children organising and making 'vehicles' and using bikes and trucks so that they could 'travel'. The two-wheeled bicycles were a great success, with many children learning to ride unaided using a complex combination of gross and fine motor skills.

Making cards and wrapping presents

At home John had always enjoyed wrapping parcels and enveloping objects with a variety of paper and fabric. He made cards to accompany his improvised presents and often gave his playgroup leader little gifts and messages. The attitude to making and giving presents in John's playgroup had been somewhat stereotypical and lacking in opportunities for individual creativity. The leader had observed John's preference for making unusual links with resources to create his constructions. As a result she allowed the children to make their own Easter cards from a range of materials. The outcomes were representational as well as abstract and all were individual, involving real design choices taken by each child. During the remainder of the year both adults and children gained confidence as they recognised the satisfaction gained from making personal decisions about shape, size, layout, choice of materials and manufacture.

Fishing

How much do teachers know about leisure time activities with which children may have become proficient? William was four-years-old. He had been in a nursery class for a term and had never spoken to an adult. He spoke at home and very occasionally to one other child in school. His father was asked what William was interested in out of school. 'He comes fishing with me,' came the reply. William blossomed as soon as his father brought his fishing gear, magazines and pictures of his 'catch' into school. Fishing magazines were then kept in the classroom and William was seen discussing pictures with other children. Designing and making fishing rods became a daily activity for a few weeks and there were many spin-offs across the curriculum. William's confidence and self-esteem grew and he became a source of interest to his peers. The teacher took time each day to listen to children talking about their interests and asked parents to reinforce discussion by bringing in artefacts, books and photographs. This link with children's home experience created additional opportunities for designing and making. For instance, Barbie was given a place in the classroom for a few weeks and her 'world' was created with custom built beds, house, castles and even a car.

Bath-time

Sophie and Millie are bath-time experts. The shared bath-time is at times a magic place, empty, calm and ready for the imagination to take over – particularly behind the white shower curtain! At other times it becomes a scientific experience. The girls mix 'potions' from shampoo, toothpaste and shower-gel – valuable exploration of liquid viscosity and miscible qualities. They use vessels for pouring, displacing, floating and sinking, developing an intuitive feel for density, upthrust and balanced forces. Bubbles are blown and hair floats out long and luxurious on the surface of the water. The two children share their fantasy and scientific worlds through talk and imitation. The learning opportunities are extended by the children's parents, who discuss, play and provide additional resources. This activity is supported in a local nursery school, where water is seen as an integral part of children's play. The role-play area is divided into three sections with a fully functioning sink and cold water tap in the kitchen area. Use of water enhances the children's play and allows for 'real' household management situations (and 'kitchen sink dramas'!) to be played out.

In one village playgroup the outdoor area is small but the opportunities for play are varied and are adapted to the particular interests of the children. Wellington boots are available at all times and we observed children constructing a waterway with a range of improvised pipes and tubing that would enable small plastic animals to drop into a bowl of blue water. They needed an appreciation that water would flow downhill as a result of gravity, and that it could easily leak out between gaps in the aqueduct they were designing and building. Play with water fed into other areas of the curriculum with a survey of the uses of water in children's homes and a full discussion about the necessity of water for life and living processes.

The sand pit

Not all children will have experienced play with sand before starting school, nursery or playgroup. It is easy to make assumptions about children's play opportunities and to assume that they will have all been on holiday to the seaside. The staff, children and parents from one primary school had spent time in thinking and consulting to find ways to improve children's use of the playground. A large sand pit had been constructed and was used randomly, on a class basis and then most effectively by mixed older and younger class groups. One Tuesday Year 6 put up a notice to invite Reception children to join them. The resultant play, construction, dialogue and co-operation provided evidence of the power of social interaction. Jason (Year 6) and Daniel (Reception) tunnelled in the sand to a depth that allowed other children to pass wheeled vehicles through. There was important discussion of the possibility of a collapse, stability, the state of the sand, the intrusion of others and possibilities for future meetings. The Reception children returned to their class and a group of them carried on their tunnelling in the class sand tray.

Building 'dens'

Blessings is five-years-old. He lives in Malawi in Central Africa, in a mud brick, thatched house in the savannah bush region high above Lake Malawi. On one occasion he appeared from the long grass with four long poles and some leaves. He tried hard to force the sticks into the baked earth but with little success. As he placed leaves between them to form a roof they collapsed under the weight. His attempt at house-building failed because he lacked help to improve the building conditions. The story of Blessings was told to children in a Year 1 class who were working on the QCA D&T unit 1D, Houses and Homes (QCA/DfEE 1998b). They saw photographs of the house in which Blessings lived and asked why he could not have used water to soften the ground for his own building. The answer was that his distance from the lake meant that water was to be used only for drinking and cooking. This led the children to design homes using locally available materials that would not require much water in the construction process. They started by making bricks from red clay, leaving some to dry naturally in the sun and firing others in a kiln. This interest had been generated from a personal story and the resultant thatched houses sparked off a longer interest in African countries with contributions from home and from the wider environment. Design and technological skills became firmly embedded in a project about human beings, their survival and their need for shelter.

Summary

As we have seen above, educational settings where children's prior scientific and technological experiences and spontaneous interest are taken into account give careful attention to how children learn in these areas and to the need for close links between home and school. Parents need to be welcomed into their child's class and invited to support scientific and D&T learning in the home. Interestingly, the booklets which schools give to parents are often concerned with the ways in which they can help children to fit into the school environment. Perhaps schools now need to consider the ways we can learn from the experiences that children are having in the home.

Parents and teachers should be co-educators. There needs to be a dialogue between them for the development of a shared understanding of the learning process. Practitioners should not set themselves up as experts but rather as partners in the learning process. They can learn so much by listening to children, responding carefully and giving children time to formulate their ideas and carry out their plans. This is particularly true of areas such as science and D&T, where few can claim to be 'experts' so there is a need to learn together. There needs to be acknowledgement that the only 'inhibiting factors are the restrictions imposed by the attending adults' (Sweet 1996: 275). Sweet draws our attention to the compliant nature of children and their desire to please. For example, Tom when he was six-years-old brought home an 'egg box daffodil' card for Easter. I thanked him and asked him if he had made it. 'No I just stuck bits in the right place,' he said. 'How did you know which was the right place?' I asked. 'Well I made my daffodil look sideways and the teacher moved the pieces to where she wanted them.' 'Why did she do that?' I replied. Tom looked straight at me and said, 'They have to look all the same.' Sweet stresses that teachers need to guard against this by adopting a 'hands off' policy that avoids the adult doing and the child watching. The temptation for practitioners in the current climate is to set clear learning objectives and predetermined outcomes for tasks. Perhaps we need to give more attention to the scientific and technological skills, knowledge and understanding that children are acquiring in the wider environment before and beyond the classroom. Then we can allow children's individual experiences to contribute to the collective learning in our particular setting.

CHAPTER 4

Using narrative to support young children's learning in science and D&T

Pat Black and Sue Hughes

Purpose of this chapter

Through reading this chapter you will gain an understanding of

- the fundamental role of narrative – including scientific and technological 'stories' – in human culture
- the importance of 'storying' as part of a spontaneous process of child–adult interaction from birth
- techniques for developing narratives to support children's learning in science and D&T.

Introduction

In Chapters 2 and 3 we have emphasised that children are motivated from birth to act upon the world (i.e. engage in designing and making) in order to make sense of it. Through actions and experiences of the senses, including shared experiences and purposes with other human beings, their scientific understanding of their environment – human, natural and made – will develop. In this chapter we intend to develop one aspect of the interactionist view of learning discussed in Chapter 2, namely that children's scientific and designerly thinking is best supported through using *narratives* – personal, cultural, traditional, contemporary, oral and printed. We shall suggest that narratives are essential to human experience, and that scientific and designerly concepts, skills and attitudes may be passed down through and exchanged within the narratives of the culture. Added to this is our belief that scientific accounts of the world – human, natural and made – can be expressed through 'explanatory stories' (Millar and Osborne 1998) and that greater use of the narrative form could be used to present scientific responses to questions regularly asked by children. The construction of narratives is an early and spontaneous process in adult–child interactions. We will argue that in these early exchanges children first encounter, make links and are inducted into methods of thinking relating to science and D&T.

Narratives in rhymes, songs and stories, first shared in the home, can be developed in the classroom to provide meaningful starting points for scientific and D&T activities. We shall explore the use of traditional and folk tales, myths and legends to develop cross-curricular work under the heading of communication, language and literacy. It was noted in Chapter 2 that children's ability to blur the boundaries between fantasy and reality in their play can be maximised to support their designing and making. When this fantasy element is introduced through a story we greatly enhance the imaginative possibilities. To illustrate these points we shall draw on cameos and case studies of children at home and school.

Narrative and culture

Although much has been written about the pivotal role language plays in teaching and learning (including that of science and D&T), the potential of narrative as a powerful vehicle or tool for learning is often overlooked and undervalued. Bruner (1990: 77) provides a detailed and compelling analysis of narrative's critical role in the development of meaning: 'I have been at great pains to argue . . . that one of the most ubiquitous and powerful discourse forms in human communication is *narrative*.' Throughout this chapter we will discuss narrative as a vehicle or tool for supporting children's thinking and thus their potential as scientists, designers and technologists. We will include narratives that are cultural and personal, traditional and contemporary, oral as well as published.

Narrative is central to children's experiences at home, at school and in the wider community. This is not limited to language; children are surrounded by and exist in a world of settings, characters and events. From a very early age children hear all sorts of narratives involving themselves, their families and their community. The narratives told by the parents or caregivers that involve the child as the principal character are perhaps most powerful in developing her understanding of the world. Whitehead (1997: 89) suggests that narratives are essential to human existence and that they are created by human beings as a means of making meaningful patterns in life and interpreting experiences that they or their ancestors, near or distant, may have had: 'At its most elemental, narrative begins with the urge to tell stories about an event, person or feeling. Narrating may even be the oldest and most basic human-language activity.' She adds that the drive to tell 'endless stories' is concerned with 'explaining, gossiping and speculating about human behaviour and the chances of life'. Narrative can therefore be viewed as a basic human-language activity, essential to daily life; a form of communicating meaning from individual to individual, community to community and from generation to generation. Mercer (2000) provides powerful illustrations of how culture and communication are inextricably linked: a community has a shared history, a collective identity, reciprocal obligations and a discourse. The function of narrative has been to act as a powerful means through which shared knowledge and understanding of self and the community, present, past and future, is developed. Rogoff (1990) argues that the cognitive activities of individuals are embedded within a cultural context. Values and skills thought to be worthy by the community constitute a 'cultural legacy' inherited from near and distant ancestors, with the assistance of caregivers and peers. She suggests that, through 'cultural institutions, technologies and traditions', problems of the present that may need solving are set; tools to assist problem solving are provided and efforts to solve problems are channelled in ways valued by the culture. Language, she suggests, is a cultural tool, which organises 'thought processes that are utilised in individuals' problem-solving and practised in institutional activities such as schooling'.

However, even within the same culture, cognitive activities such as problem solving may be influenced by values specific to the context. For example, learning about food production through designing and making a pizza may be thought of as worthwhile within both the cultural institutions of school and home. The language tool for this activity may consist of a recipe (a culturally organised procedural text) plus verbal instruction to support the text. Adults' values, relating to food either in the home or the school, may be influenced by past or present circumstances. In either of these institutions learning through making mistakes – for example, burning the pizza – may be thought acceptable and a valuable part of the learning experience, but the issue of wasted ingredients may be differently expressed through verbal disapproval. Whether acceptable or unacceptable, factual or embellished, between peers or family, it is likely that a 'narrative' of the experience will develop and will be a contributing factor to the child's learning process.

Narratives, then, are essential to human existence and are used within a culture to communicate an understanding of the culture's past and present, as well as its predicted future: 'Narratives may be a crucial element in human evolution and intelligent adaptability, enabling the species to predict or make up stories about likely outcomes as well as remote possibilities' (Whitehead 1997: 91). Some of the most powerful narratives about the past, present and future of Western society are those presented by scientists, technologists and designers. Our current understanding of human evolution, the influence of biotechnology on us as a species, and the utopian or doomsday scenarios of our hi-tech or environmentally catastrophic futures, all emanate from these professions. So it should come as no surprise that narrative plays an important part in their work.

Stories used by designers, technologists and scientists

Designers sometimes use narrative to gain understandings of their clients' lifestyles and needs (Davies 1996). In the early stages of a project, a designer might envisage the type of person who is likely to use the product in question and invent simple narratives to describe the situations in which they might make use of it. This is known as 'human factors' research:

We think about all the steps a person will go through as they use a product: how they will get started; what they have to do while they use it; and how they stop and put it away. Sometimes we write or draw these sequences to remember them. For each step we think about what the important human factors are.

(interviewed human factors designer)

Mercer (2000: 110–11) suggests that the use of narratives as a way of communicating key information is prevalent in industry. He suggests that those working in industry 'spend most of their time telling each other "stories" . . . (for these) are a means for displaying experience and expertise, provide "models" for doing the shared action in which the partners are engaged, and communicate technical knowledge in a memorable form'. Many of the stories technicians share are based on told or learned knowledge about how the world works and may include tales of work, family and community: 'In the community . . . telling relevant stories about dealing with past problems is a way of thinking together' (Mercer 2000: 111). For young children, giving a running commentary about what they are making in the construction area, or telling an adult about the teddy for whom they are designing a hat, may fulfil some of the same narrative functions.

Scientists too have their own narratives, which have been constructed to offer explanations of the world, its inhabitants and the environment, natural or made. These narratives change over time as knowledge and understanding increase. For example, most people once believed that the world was flat and that the Earth was the centre of the universe. Through the work of scientists including Copernicus and Gallileo in the sixteenth and seventeenth centuries these understandings changed to a view of the Sun as the centre of the universe with a spherical Earth orbiting it. Later scientists realised that the Sun itself was orbiting the Milky Way Galaxy, and Einstein in the twentieth century introduced the idea that the universe has no centre, since all motion is relative. Recent work by cosmologists and physicists including Stephen Hawking suggest an expanding universe (or universes!), complete with a Big Bang, black holes, dark matter and many other strange phenomena. There is an insatiable public appetite for popular science books and television documentaries propounding the latest versions of competing stories about our place in the universe.

This form of narrative has implications for practitioners in all phases of education. Millar and Osborne (1998: 13) suggest that 'science education should make greater use of one of the world's most powerful and pervasive ways of communicating ideas – the narrative form'. They recommend that science education should present scientific knowledge as a number of key 'explanatory stories' (see also Harlen 2000: 25) and that children need to approach these stories 'not as "given" knowledge but as the product of sustained inquiry by individuals working in social and historical contexts'. The examples they give of such explanatory stories include the Earth and beyond (above) and the particle model of matter:

Imagine being able to 'peek inside' matter. Then you would 'see' that matter is made of tiny particles of less than 100 different types. These particles, called atoms, move about, arranging or re-arranging themselves in patterns or sticking together to make new, more complex particles. Alternatively, complex particles can be broken up into their constituent atoms.

(Millar and Osborne 1998: 14)

This important idea, from which many ways of understanding phenomena such as mixing, dissolving and burning derive, is really a story in that we don't know whether it is 'true' or not. Dalton's original hypothesis about atoms, made at the beginning of the nineteenth century, has found much support from experimental evidence and led to all sorts of other ideas such as quantum theory, but the fact remains that nobody has ever actually 'seen' an atom! This is an important characteristic of science that we believe it is important for children to grasp; namely that science tells us great stories to help us understand our surroundings, but they are not 'facts' and will almost certainly change in the telling. The National Curriculum for science (DfEE/QCA 1999b) reflects this in its inclusion of a section entitled 'Ideas and Evidence in Science' under the heading of Scientific Enquiry. This invites children to look at powerful ideas, such as Jenner's understanding of antibodies that led to early vaccination, through stories of scientists' work and the evidence they have used – another example of using narrative in teaching and learning science. For children in the Early Years, most will have recent experience of 'having an injection'. We can use this experience to begin to tell the explanatory story about our bodies' defences against disease. What does it feel like to be ill? Why do we need to have injections? Have any children felt a 'little bit' ill after having an injection and why do they think this is? Setting up the role-play area as a doctor's surgery where children can go and 'have an injection' will spark numerous recollections and acted-out stories related to vaccination.

Personal narratives or 'storying'

Let us now turn our attention to *personal narratives* and their function in developing children's thinking in early childhood. The term 'storying' is used by Whitehead (1997: 92) to describe personal narratives shared between young children and their caregivers in early interactions between them. She uses this term as a way of distinguishing 'personal narrative activity from the published or traditional stories current in a community'. Can shared personal narratives contribute to children's learning in science and D&T? We suggest that as children begin formal education, narratives can act as a bridge, spanning and connecting children's early knowledge and understanding of science and D&T to versions of these subjects that they will experience in school, nursery or playgroup (see Chapter 2). This early knowledge and understanding has been gained through early interaction and shared personal narratives with caregivers: 'In the first two years of life it is the people constantly with the baby who tell most of the stories' (Whitehead 1997: 96). These narratives are 'basic and spontaneous' and are not to be confused with published forms. However, elements of published cultural narratives may be included in the story being told.

For example, when dressing a young child in a red coat the caregiver's narrative may proceed as follows:

> We're getting ready to go to the big shops. We need to get lots of food for Holly's party. We need to put on your coat and go in the car and be back in time for Holly coming out of school. Holly likes you in your red coat, doesn't she? She calls you 'Little Red Riding Hood' and pretends to be the wolf.

Trevarthen (1995) suggests that children are born expecting to communicate and share meaningful experiences with caregivers. His research found that from birth children have a desire to communicate and actively seek to 'chat' with caregivers, thus beginning the 'narrative' of communication between them. In these early 'conversations' both participants take active roles and mutually encourage each other. In the example of the conversation above, while the adult talks to the child, the child too would be contributing through eye-contact, smiles, gestures and vocalisations, thus encouraging the adult to continue. Through such exchanges, young children 'eagerly learn the language and all other peculiar habits and beliefs of our community'. These 'habits and beliefs' of their culture include those relating to scientific and designerly activities and thinking, such as the importance of planning what we will make or do. The following four short cameos of a young child at play illustrate how early storying contributes to the development of scientific and designerly thinking.

Cameo 1: Identifying and classifying animals

Through storying shared with him in play, Yorgi (16 months) is refining his already developing scientific skills and concepts. When playing with his toy animals he is skilled at classifying them through the 'sounds' they make. These sounds have been internalised by him though stories read to him about animals and those shared with him when playing alongside his animal toys. For example, farm animals are identified and classified according to his perception of their type. Sheep-like animals say, 'bah, bah', cow-like say 'moo', pig-like make a remarkable nasal grunt. Wild animals are also categorised in this way: 'rawagh, rawagh' mimicking a lion for all big cats, 'hoo, hoo' for a monkey, and an upward arm movement with very little accompanying sound represents elephants. Vehicles used for transporting the animals, as with all machinery (including the vacuum and coffee maker) of course, are represented by the sound, 'mmmm, mmmm'. When systematically arranging the habitat of his wild animals, he is developing an awareness that the giraffes and zebras cannot possibly be housed with the 'big cats' without serious consequences. The shared storying has told him so. Through visiting zoos this concept will be developed: animals will be housed according to classification, and the personal narratives shared with the adults that accompany the visits will confirm this. Through nature programmes on television (a type of cultural narrative) the characteristics of the natural habitats for each of these animals will be revealed, together with their feeding relationships.

Cameo 2: The night sky

Through observing the night sky with adults, Yorgi is able to identify the moon and stars. On seeing them he automatically rocks backwards and forwards in a rhythmic movement accompanied by his 'singing' to encourage his caregiver to share the rhyme 'Twinkle, twinkle little star' and the song 'I see the moon'. Trevarthen (1995) describes this type of interaction between child and caregiver as a 'rhythmic story' which has all the features of a narrative, including 'an intro-duction, build-up, climax and resolution'. Given Yorgi's response to the night sky, we might ask why the Earth and beyond is not introduced until Key Stage 2 in the National Curriculum.

Cameo 3: Building and making

Yorgi shares with his caregiver his new developing skill of building with commer-cially produced interlocking bricks. As the physical skill of building is practised, habitats are created to house toy people and soft animals. 'Bob the Builder', along with a policeman and fireman from the set of bricks, have various adventures that require structures and equipment made from the bricks. With each adventure is an accompanying 'story'. The picnic bench has to be made longer for all three figures to be seated. Yorgi, when seeing a tall tower with 'Bob' on the top will put his hands up to his mouth and exclaim, 'Oh no!', knowing that from past experi-ences and the shared stories, 'Bob' will soon suffer the consequences of a tower design lacking in safety features!

Cameo 4: Arranging the home for the 'new baby'

Through recent changes to his home in preparation for a younger brother, Yorgi shares with his parents the many narratives about 'his new baby'. When members of the extended family visit, he is able to take them upstairs to explain and report (through vocalising and many arm gestures) the new order of his and his baby's bedrooms. In each room he directs his hands and arms with accompanying long vocalisations, as he exchanges the 'stories' of the possible positions for soon-to-arrive new furniture. At the mention of the word 'wardrobe' he immediately takes up a position in the corner of his bedroom and gestures and laughs. As he 'assists' in arranging and rearranging his clothes and soft toys into various temporary con-tainers the narrative between him and his mother includes the benefits and dis-advantages of these items being placed in easy and difficult to reach locations.

Commentary

What, then, do the above cameos tell us about the development of designerly and scientific thinking through personal narratives with young children? In cameos 1 and 2, Yorgi is developing the essential scientific skills of observation and classifica-tion. In some senses these skills are 'natural' and pre-programmed, but by telling stories as he does them, and incorporating elements of the cultural narratives that surround him, they become much more powerful. In cameos 3 and 4 his understanding of the 'client' (be it Bob the Builder or his baby brother) developed through storying makes his designerly behaviour (joining and arranging elements) more meaningful. As Early Years practitioners we need to remember to utilise and maximise this basic and spontaneous form of narrative to develop, refine and expand children's thinking.

Opportunities that arise spontaneously need to be recognised as potential learning experiences and incorporated into daily classroom activities. For example, children arrive at school unprepared and very wet after a sudden deluge. After sharing in their stories of how and why they got so wet this situation becomes a 'natural' starting point for investigations of materials that are waterproof, designing clothes to protect body, legs and feet. Opportunities that adults have planned can be purposeful and include children's recollections (stories), views and designs. For example, rearranging the classroom provides opportunities for discussions with children about possible design and layout of furniture, and for sharing stories of how it was and how it could be improved – 'human factor' research with teacher and children as designers and clients.

Using cultural narratives as starting points

What, therefore, are the cultural narratives that are significant to children and how can they be used to support children's thinking in science, design and technology? The cultural narratives that are of most significance to children are the nursery rhymes and songs, traditional and folk tales, myths and legends, originally told orally and now fixed in print. Added to oral and published narratives are those increasingly important narratives within the media of television and films.

Using stories as starting points for science and D&T is an established feature of primary practice, and several publications have been produced over recent years to support teachers in planning for this. For example, the *Collins Primary Science* scheme (Howe 1990) uses traditional tales and rhymes as starting points for a range of scientific activities. In *Threads of Thinking* (1999), Cathy Nutbrown explores the notion of 'Nourishing children's thinking through stories'. Using *The Tooth Ball* (Pearce 1987) as a starting point, Nutbrown describes how, 'after telling this story to her class of 5-year-olds, a teacher introduced some work on wrapping and packaging' (1999: 87). The Design Council produced a video resource pack *Stories as Starting Points for Design and Technology* (1991) and several local education authorities, including Lewisham (1999), have published guidelines on using literature to support learning across the curriculum, including science:

> Fiction can provide a context and therefore a reason for developing scientific skills, attitudes and concepts. Stories and poems can be used to stimulate questions which can be explored further, e.g. *The Iron Man* as a stimulus for work on magnetism or *Mr Gumpy's Outing* to explore floating and sinking.
>
> (Lewisham Education and Culture 1999: 113)

Table 4.1: Stories as starting points for D&T and science

Title	Author(s) and publisher	Science links	Needs/Wants (D&T)
The Lighthouse Keeper's Lunch	Ronda and David Armitage, Scholastic	Humans – nutrition	Something to protect and scare birds A packed lunch
Who Sank The Boat?	Pamela Allen, Puffin	Forces – floating and sinking	A boat that will carry some animals without sinking
Owl at Home	Arnold Lobel, Mammoth	Materials	A house to keep the winter out Something to get Owl up and down stairs quickly
Mr Gumpy's Outing	John Burningham, Puffin	Forces – floating and sinking	A boat to carry all the passengers without sinking
Whatever Next!	Jill Murphy, Picture Mac	Forces, Earth and beyond	A rocket like Baby Bear's, to go to the moon
Good-night Owl!	Pat Hutchins, Puffin	Sound	A sound-proof house for Owl
Jim and the Beanstalk	Raymond Briggs, Puffin	Life and living processes	New teeth, glasses and a wig for the giant
Peace at Last	Jill Murphy, Macmillan	Sound	Ear muffs for Father Bear
Can't You Sleep Little Bear?	Martin Wadell, Walker Books	Light	A light for Little Bear's cave

For D&T, stories offer the opportunity to identify with a character and empathise with his or her needs. For example, in Raymond Briggs's *Jim and the Beanstalk*, the giant has poor eyesight, little hair and no teeth. This provides the opportunity for pupils to design glasses, wigs and false teeth for these 'fantasy' needs, a project undertaken by the Reception class at Trinity Primary School in Taunton. Examples of stories in which the characters have clearly identifiable needs are given in Table 4.1, which also shows how the same stories could be used to support scientific learning.

Learning 'embedded' in a familiar cultural context both stimulates and extends children's deeper understanding. Narrative provides a wonderfully supportive framework for young children's learning, as Berger (1997: 29) in his exploration of narrative explains:

> When we are dealing with concepts, notions, or ideas, we make sense of them by contrasting them with their opposites, that is why when we read or hear the word *rich*, we automatically contrast it with *poor*, and when we read or hear the word *happy* we think of the word *sad*. If everyone has a great deal of money *rich* loses its meaning; *rich* means something only in contrast to *poor*.

Through such stories and rhymes young children gain an enormous amount of knowledge about how things work: permanent and reversible changes, the effect of gravity, properties of materials. Young children are inspired to explore scientific theories and design problems inherent in such narratives: the 'basic and spontaneous' become opportunities for embedded tasks (Donaldson 1978). In the following case study a traditional tale was used to instigate real scientific discovery and technological solutions.

Case study: Material from traditional tales

Judy Cooper, Year 1 class teacher at Broad Chalke CE First School, Wiltshire, describes her work with 'The Three Little Pigs':

'As a starting point the children went on a walk around the village to observe houses in terms of their materials and different styles. They were able to identify similarities and differences. The walk enabled the children to discuss building materials with confidence. The story of "The Three Little Pigs" was very much enjoyed. They worked in groups to build houses which were then tested to see if they could be blown down.'

Judy brought literacy and science together to very powerful effect. As can be seen from the teaching objectives for this unit of work (Table 4.2), reading, writing, speaking and listening activities informed and inspired activity in science and vice versa.

The children followed the Three Little Pigs in their search for a 'safe house'. From this concrete example of the need for selecting the 'best' material children were supported in their more abstract investigation of materials. Had the children been asked to compare the properties of materials without the background of the pigs' dilemma, they may have found it difficult to articulate difference and similarity. The weakness of the straw used by the first little pig provides an extreme example against which the children can measure other materials. The story itself and the conversation arising from its reading can prompt new descriptions which can be used for further exploration and discovery.

In this Year 1 classroom the display boards and cupboard tops reflected the learning of the children. In order to design their own 'dream homes' and avoid the disaster that struck the homes of the first two pigs the children researched and tested materials, looked at the shape and features of houses and tried out their theories on houses made by the class. Having completed their investigation the

Table 4.2: Learning outcomes for science and literacy from 'The Three Little Pigs'

Literacy	Science
Traditional Stories	*Observation, Description and Exploration of Materials*
To extend vocabulary; develop ideas and opinions; to collect words associated with houses.	Name and describe the building materials used in 'The Three Little Pigs'.
Record observations from sorting materials into sets, e.g. hard/soft, rough/smooth, weak/strong.	Mind map knowledge of houses and the materials used for building.
Children to talk about their own homes, using photographs brought in as stimulus.	Gather evidence of features and materials of homes in the local area from an observation trail.
Share the story of 'The Three Little Pigs'. Use the story as a stimulus to raise the question of suitability of different materials for building a house.	Explore and describe a collection of building materials using appropriate senses.
Use reference books and evidence from observation to discover different types of homes and materials used to build them and record findings.	Explore and recognise similarities and differences in building materials.
Write sentences using 'I saw . . .' sentence structure to describe features of houses and materials used in building.	Investigate and test the suitability of materials for building a house.
Record science investigation – testing materials.	Use straw, sticks and bricks to build three houses and then try to blow them down. Reinforce work on forces from last term. Use hair dryer for increasing force.
Design own home using information for investigation, observation, research and discussion.	

Figure 4.1: Making a house as part of a topic on 'The Three Little Pigs'

children were then able to apply their understanding to design and make their own houses (Figure 4.1).

Commentary

Not only did this traditional tale provide an ideal starting point for young children's work on materials, it enabled the teacher to bring in other aspects of their scientific understanding and apply them creatively to current learning. The effects of forces on materials may be a complex concept for six-year-olds but they are very familiar with the repeated chant of the wolf as he huffs and puffs and blows houses down.

Summary

This chapter has restated the primacy of narrative in children's learning about themselves, the cultures they inhabit and the physical environments they explore. Learning in science and D&T involves 'telling stories', whether the spontaneous narratives that develop between parent and child or the more structured forms of narrative involved in describing a sequence of stages in making or explaining the development of a scientific idea over time. We have explored ways in which Early Years practitioners can exploit this interplay between culture, literacy, science and design through discussing children's personal narratives and by using traditional tales or rhymes as starting points. These themes will be picked up and developed in subsequent chapters.

CHAPTER 5

Assessing young children's learning in science and D&T

Alan Howe and Kendra McMahon

Purpose of this chapter

Through reading this chapter, you will gain

- an overview of the relevance of assessment to Early Years education
- an understanding of what to look for when observing and assessing science and D&T
- A range of strategies for use in assessing and recording young children's progress in these areas.

Introduction: the relevance of assessment to Early Years education

Books about teaching and learning tend to place the assessment chapter near the end, almost as an afterthought or 'necessary evil'. Assessment is at the centre of this book, because we believe that it is a wholly integral part of learning and teaching. Early Years practitioners are constantly making judgements about what to do next when supporting children's learning – which experiences to offer, how to act, what to say. The expertise to make such judgements depends on a good knowledge of the learner's mind, which can only be gained through assessment *for* learning, also known as *formative* (i.e. 'informing') assessment or *elicitation* (see Chapter 2). Ollerenshaw and Ritchie (1997) point out that elicitation also has a *metacognitive* dimension. It can help the learner understand something about their own learning processes as ideas are explored and changes in thinking are identified.

In practice these ideas about learning demand that we make a serious effort to find out what children already know and can do. We must, therefore, plan opportunities that encourage children to expose their thinking and demonstrate their capabilities. However, assessment can occur at any point of the learning process; we need to monitor children's progress *during* their learning, and 'sum it up' at the end – *summative* assessment or assessment *of* learning. The Assessment Reform Group (1999) point out that if assessment is to be effective it should not happen on an *ad hoc* basis; teachers should decide how and when to assess pupils' attainment at the same time as they plan the work. We include examples of this below, and in Chapter 7.

In our experience assessment can easily be misunderstood. Simplified and relatively crude assessment has tended to dominate in recent years in attempts to generate data that can be used in comparative exercises. If assessment is not purposeful and informative to the practitioner it becomes onerous and may seem irrelevant. We need constantly to ask ourselves, 'How does this help the child in his or her learning?' Assessment is not the same as taking measurements. We can measure a child's height easily – it is a one-dimensional activity. Assessing a child's learning is much more complex. If it is to be worthwhile, the process will consider the child from a variety of perspectives and over a period of time. *It is about getting to know the child as a learner.*

Before we proceed we must also add a note of caution. Worthwhile assessment takes time, as does recording and reporting the results of assessment. Evidence suggests that it is not easy to get right. Ofsted (2000: para. 33) note that

> in almost half of all (900 observed Early Years) settings, staff do not assess children's attainment and progress effectively. For example, staff do not record their observations of children's responses to activities, or, if such observations are recorded, they are not used to identify particular learning needs, and to help inform future planning.

In the primary sector, Ofsted (2001a: para. 25) report that:

> the quality and use of assessment remain the weakest aspect of teaching. Many schools are generating a great deal of assessment data, at considerable cost in terms of time, but are not using it to set work based on the pupils' prior attainment or to set appropriate targets for different groups of pupils.

The key message seems to be that we need to *use* our assessments of children's learning to inform 'the next step' in planning and teaching. This is never easy or clear-cut, though we do make some suggestions as to possible 'next steps' in this and subsequent chapters. We need to remember, however, that assessment can have other purposes too: to inform parents on their children's progress, to diagnose specific needs, to evaluate practice in order to inform more strategic planning for the development of provision and staff development and to satisfy the demands of accountability. We will touch upon each of these aspects in this chapter, but need to start with what we consider the most appropriate purpose for assessment in Early Years science and D&T – to inform our practice.

What do we assess?

Perhaps the aspect of assessment requiring most skill is that of identifying significant moments or comments. This requires the practitioner to be familiar with expectations of children's learning such as those set out in the Early Learning Goals (ELG) (QCA/DfEE 2000) and National Curriculum and to have a sense of progression in children's science and D&T learning. We need to assess children's attitudes, skills and conceptual understanding in both areas, although in practice these strands may be difficult to disentangle. In the Foundation Stage, attitudes that children may develop in science and D&T contexts are summarised within the area of learning dealing with personal, social and emotional development (see Chapter 6 for a fuller exploration of these areas). The area 'Knowledge and Understanding of the World' includes the ELG:

Investigate objects and materials by using all their senses as appropriate.

This goal, as with other ELGs, mixes the enquiry skills we are looking for with children's developing knowledge and understanding, necessitating a 'holistic' approach to assessment (see Chapter 1). ELGs are reached by progress along 'stepping stones' (QCA/DfEE 2000). Although this analogy would seem to suggest that children attain the goals through a linear series of steps, 'not all children conform so neatly to this sequence of learning . . . Some will have appeared to have been achieved very quickly, others will take much longer' (QCA/DfEE 2000: 27). In other words, some children may 'skip' some steps, or dwell for some time upon others. The flexible nature of *Curriculum Guidance for the Foundation Stage* gives the practitioner the opportunity to adjust planning to take account of these different rates of progress, and of children's enthusiasms and interests.

Assessing science and D&T at Key Stage 1

As suggested in Chapter 1, the divide between learning at the Foundation Stage and Key Stage 1 is somewhat artificial. Nevertheless, in statutory terms, the teacher has a very different task to perform with children in Years 1 and 2. That is not to say that formative assessment is any less crucial; QCA (2002) continues to emphasise this in its guidance to schools, using the term 'teacher assessment' to include both formative and summative assessment.

Science

The Key Stage 1 teacher has to consider assessment of both scientific enquiry (Sc1 – essentially skills-based) and Sc2, 3 and 4 (essentially knowledge-based). In typical school planning cycles, children are unlikely to revisit any specific area of scientific knowledge during the same academic year. There is a number of implications of this in relation to assessment and planning. If assessment of knowledge and understanding is to be formative then it will need to be done soon enough to allow the class teacher to adjust planning *during* the unit of work. In some cases it would be ideal to conduct some elicitation activity before a detailed weekly plan has been drawn up, so the teacher is fully informed about the children's prior knowledge. Records from previous years will be useful in showing what the group or class had 'covered' and understood at the time, but such records are unlikely to give sufficiently detailed insights into children's understanding as it stood some months or even years ago. Assessment of knowledge and understanding at the end of a topic or unit can only be summative in nature unless the next topic is closely linked. On the other hand, children's enquiry skills will develop each time they do science, so assessment of skills can be more easily 'carried forward' to the next unit or medium-term plan.

The QCA/DfEE *Scheme of Work* for science (1998a) identifies summative 'expectations' for each unit at three levels; some teachers use these to compile lists of children who have met each set of criteria. The scheme also identifies some formative strategies in the 'activities' sections. For example in unit 1f: Sound and Hearing, it is suggested that a teacher starts a lesson by asking children to draw a picture or describe how they think we hear, before engaging them in some activities to help them understand the ear's function in hearing.

The National Curriculum for science (DfEE/QCA 1999b) gives us four 'Attainment Targets' (ATs), which are intended for summative use, with the expectation that most children will reach Level 2 across the ATs by the end of Year 2. They are designed to be applied using a 'best fit' method, in which teachers consider descriptions for adjacent levels before making a final judgement. Stringer (1996) has converted the programmes of study into 'childspeak' statements that allow the teacher and the child to make joint judgements about progress and attainment. For example, the National Curriculum requirement that children 'should be taught to use first hand experience and simple information sources to answer questions' (Sc1, 2b) has been converted to 'I can learn from what I can do and from what I read, listen to and watch.' Di Buck and Helen Diles from Bristol LEA have taken the idea one step further and produced a 'levelled' set of scientific enquiry statements (Table 5.1). Again the intention is for child and teacher to be involved in setting targets and assessing progress summatively.

Unfortunately, children's scientific attitudes do not feature in the ATs. Assessing attitudes is complex and very much dependent on context – we can all lack curiosity if the topic simply doesn't turn us on. When using Table 5.1, teachers may wish to add an attitudinal dimension to their assessment. If it seems that children are not 'turned on' by the science in their class some significant rethinking of the provision for science may need to be considered.

Design & technology

The National Curriculum (DfEE/QCA 1999c) and accompanying scheme of work (QCA/DfEE 1998b) provide us with a starting point for 'what to assess' in D&T. Here we have one attainment target, which combines the skills of designing, making and evaluating products. There is less of a tradition of assessing children's prior knowledge in D&T than in science, although this is no less relevant if a particular unit will require children to draw on knowledge which the teacher is assuming the class have already encountered. Focused Practical Tasks (FPTs – see Chapter 10) can serve as elicitation activities; for example an activity to construct frames using construction kits in Unit 1B: Playgrounds could serve the dual purpose of sharing ideas

Table 5.1: Children's self-assessment of Attainment Target 1: Scientific Enquiry

Progression in scientific enquiry	Planning	Getting the evidence	Using the evidence
Level 1	I can talk about the things I need with my teacher.	I can use equipment with help. I can explore objects, living things and events with all my senses.	I can describe what I have explored.
Level 2	I can think of ways of finding things out. I can use texts to find information that I need.	I can use equipment with help. I can talk about what has happened and I can make and record observations using drawings, tables pictograms or block graphs.	I can compare objects, living things and events. I can describe observations clearly and use simple tables. I can say if what happened was what I expected.
Level 3	I can suggest my own ways of finding things out. I can say what I think will happen. I understand why it is important to collect information to answer questions.	I can carry out a fair test with some help. I can use simple equipment to test, observe and measure. I can record my findings in a variety of ways.	I can describe simple patterns in my results. I can explain what has happened using scientific language. I can see how to improve my results. I understand what makes a test fair or unfair.

Source: Helen Diles, Bristol LEA (with permission)

for making stable structures, while giving the teacher an insight into the levels of understanding within the class. During a Design and Make Assignment (DMA – see Chapter 10) the teacher may notice that children are not thinking about using materials economically, or are finding it difficult to choose the appropriate tool for the job – assessments which should lead to appropriate interventions.

Ritchie (2001) suggests that assessment in D&T is likely to be formative, go hand-in-hand with teaching, inform teacher's interventions and be ongoing throughout children's work. Howe *et al.* (2001: 38) point out that assessment is a part of children's evaluation and that an important aim in D&T should be for children to make a realistic self-evaluation of their own creative output. Children should be taught how to make honest and reflective self-evaluations of their work based on clear criteria:

> Evaluation will begin with recall and *description*. By asking children to talk about what they have done, remembering the sequence of events and incidents along the way, the process will have begun. Most teachers have had the experience of asking young children questions such as 'can you think of ways of improving your model?' and getting a firm 'no' in reply. Young children find it notoriously difficult to make such comments; they do not have a conception that what they have done may in some way be inadequate and it is unfortunate if we plant the idea that this is the case . . .

It is common practice in teaching to state clearly at the start of a lesson the learning objectives derived from curriculum requirements. Teachers will also make explicit their expectations about other aspects of classroom organisation and management – for example regarding behaviour, use of resources or group work. It is from a combination of these objectives and expectations that criteria for evaluating children's work can partly be drawn. A third source of criteria will come from the design brief and particular specifications associated with the DMA. Ideally these will have been developed through discussion and negotiation with the class. Once criteria have been established then it is important that they are revisited and that they are used. For example, our teaching objectives might be for children to learn 'to use existing fabric designs as inspiration for their own pattern-making', and 'that some tasks have to be done prior to others when involved in making' (unit 2D: Joseph's Coat). They are also expected to access their own resources in a safe and co-operative way to make a coat with a specification that the coat would fit a 20 cm doll. The evaluation must then focus on these matters. Questions resulting from the activity might include:

'How is your design like the designs we looked at?'
'What did you do first? Did you do things in the best order?'
'How did you keep safe while you worked?'
'Does your coat fit the doll? Why/why not?'

Through selecting our questions carefully we can focus our assessment and avoid the intimidating and unproductive question 'What can you do to improve this?'

In the same way that we have shown science ATs in child-friendly language to help children become involved in self-assessment, Table 5.2 shows D&T statements similarly phrased.

Table 5.2: Children's self-assessment of D&T Attainment Target

Progression in D&T	Designing	Making	Evaluating
Level 1	I can think of some ideas. I can make a plan with words and pictures.	I can talk about what I am doing. I can use some tools and materials with help.	I can talk about my work. I know about how some things work and I can tell others about them.
Level 2	I can think of my own ideas. I can use ideas from other design & technology I have done. I can use models, pictures and words to describe my designs.	I can say why I have chosen to use certain tools and materials. I can use tools and materials in different ways.	I can say what I have done well and what I have learned so I can do it better in the future.
Level 3	I have had ideas for a number of different projects. I can make realistic plans. I can tell others about my designs in detail by using words, labelled sketches and models. I can think ahead to plan my work.	I can make things quite carefully and accurately.	I can say where I have thought about and made improvements as I worked.

Assessment for learning in science and D&T

Science and D&T in the Early Years are, as we have seen, essentially practical subjects concerned with process. Therefore, formative assessment, which captures contextualised (and sometimes 'scaffolded') learning, is most appropriate for assessing these areas in the Foundation Stage and early Key Stage 1. Formative assessment can provide information of a summative nature for reporting purposes, e.g. by providing parents with 'snapshots' of episodes of learning taking place. However, this is not its primary purpose. Several strategies are of particular value in gathering the evidence upon which formative judgements can be made. We will outline several of these below using scientific examples, though most of them could be adapted for D&T.

Observation

At the heart of assessing young children's learning in science and D&T is the technique of *observation*. The importance of watching young children's actions and interactions is widely recognised by Early Years practitioners. As children get older, other assessment strategies come into play, yet observation still remains crucial to assess the ways in which children go about scientific enquiry or designing and making. When recording our observations, the information will be more contextualised if we note, *during everyday classroom activity*:

- where the child is
- who the child is with
- what the child can do alone
- what the child can do with help
- what the child says
- the length of time of interactions/non-interactions.

To gain a holistic overview of a child's capabilities, observation should be carried out over a range of science and D&T-related activities in a variety of social contexts, e.g. when the child is with an adult, or a group of peers, or working independently. Sometimes the activities should be teacher-initiated as this can provide a broader range of experiences than children may encounter on their own. At other times the observed activity should be something the child has initiated herself, because it is when she is fully engaged and interested that she may demonstrate her most creative behaviour and deep understanding. We need to plan time for observation (see Chapter 7) otherwise it is easy to become too 'caught up' in the activities to focus on particular children's learning.

Observation techniques may be broadly classified as either participant or non-participant. The latter implies that the practitioner stays outside the action – watching and listening and noting what is seen and heard without intervening. This is a very useful (although sometimes difficult) strategy with younger children who may express more through their actions than they are able to verbalise. Participant observers, by contrast, are very much part of the activity – making comments or asking questions that clarify children's actions or invite them to explore further. In this case it is more difficult to make notes at the time, so we may need to remember them for recording as soon as possible after the episode. It is particularly important that support staff, nursery nurses and other adults are involved in both these forms of observation, guided as to what to look for in science and D&T, and made to feel that their observations are valued, as in the following example.

Cameo: Reflection

After the Reception teacher's input on 'torches' in which she discusses how they work, how they can be switched on and off and how hand-held mirrors can be used to 'bounce' the light around the room, a number of children decide to play with the torches and mirrors. 'Melissa' plays on her own for the 15-minute session, looking around the room to find shiny surfaces in a systematic way that will 'bounce' her torchlight. The teacher notices that she finds a number of reflective surfaces during the explorations. At one point the child talks to a learning support assistant (LSA) and tells him of her discovery that the TV screen is 'like a mirror'. The LSA responds enthusiastically and poses a question, 'Could I check my hair in it then?'

Commentary

The LSA's observation of this behaviour provides information about the child's attitudes to exploration in science-based activities, such as her level of curiosity and her perseverance. It also raises questions: what can the teacher say about her knowledge, her vocabulary and her ability to ask and answer questions? Is more information needed? The observation might also provide evaluation evidence of the appropriateness of provision and the expertise of the learning assistant. Finally, the teacher needs to make a judgement about 'the next step' in Melissa's experience of reflection. Should she ask Melissa to tell other children about her discovery, or ask the LSA to work with her on recording her findings, perhaps with a picture or photograph?

Involvement of other adults in observation helps to provide information about how children are working in a variety of contexts and also means that judgements can be reconsidered if there are inconsistencies in what is observed by different people. It is particularly useful to enlist the help of another observer if one adult is actively involved in teaching. For example, Louise, a trainee teacher on her final school placement, led a discussion about 'things which keep us healthy' in order to elicit children's ideas. She asked her LSA to note the children's responses during the discussion. Analysis of the resultant notes confirmed Louise's impression that some children had a good prior knowledge of this topic, and also that she would need to consider another way to elicit some children's knowledge as they did not readily contribute to the class discussion. She was able to focus on these children during a later group discussion.

Recording observations to inform planning

We sometimes unwittingly use observations to confirm our existing assumptions about a child, rather than being open to learn new information about her (Fisher 1996). We need to recognise that our preconceived ideas might present barriers to our perceptions of young children's capabilities and lead us towards a 'deficit' model in which future activities are planned to address perceived weaknesses. If instead we actively seek evidence of children's achievement and unexpected expertise, our planning for future learning can take into account their individual learning styles and the kinds of experiences that will engage them, rather than simply 'plugging gaps' in children's knowledge and skills. The following case study provides examples of science planning from such 'positive' observation.

Case study: Mo Pearson at Blaise Primary School

In the nursery class at Blaise Primary School in Bristol, teacher Mo Pearson feels very strongly that it is important that she develops her planning based on the children's interests and follows up their ideas and enthusiasms. She has a clear idea of the scientific attitudes, skills and knowledge and understanding that she wants the children to develop and uses formative assessment to help her to plan opportunities for learning that meet their needs and follow their interests. In order to do this formative assessment information is gathered through observation during spontaneous play and more structured activities. The observations are important because in their actions young children show how they feel about what they are doing, show what they can do and may demonstrate a depth of understanding that they are not able to put into words. However, Mo also gains evidence of children's learning from listening to and having conversations with children:

> Even now, I find I've made assumptions (about a child's understanding) – it is so important to take time to really listen to what children say. I'm often surprised.

Mo has a clear idea of the content of the Early Learning Goals (QCA/DfEE 2000) that she carries in her head, and this informs her decisions about which of her ongoing observations are recorded as an important development for the child. Observations are then written onto a Post-it or strip of paper and stuck onto a record sheet for that child. In her class every child has a page of records for each of the areas of learning identified in the Curriculum Guidance for the Foundation Stage (QCA/DfEE 2000). It is important that these notes are both specific and succinct if they are to form a useful record of children's learning and development. The notes need to make it clear how independent the child has been in doing something and are phrased to focus on children's achievements rather than aspects they are still having difficulties with, as this sets up a positive discussion when these records are shared with parents. The children's exact words (utterances) are often noted, and the record makes it clear whether the words were part of a conversation with an adult or another child, or spoken aloud to themselves in play. Other adults in the classroom also contribute to these records, which are dated and explain the context of the observation. This is important as the child may respond differently when ideas are presented in a different context according to how meaningful that particular situation is to them at that time.

In the extract from 'Heather's' record (Figure 5.1) there are examples of how she compared the feel of materials in different contexts, including a one-to-one discussion with her teacher about a display of tactile materials and as noted in spon-

Tactile Display. (asked "what does it feel like?") intro. said without prompting
"it's soft" touching material
"a big, hard one" touching cork square
"these are sprinkly"   "   shredded paper
"that feels crunchy"   "   cellophane
recognised some materials felt different when asked to compare 2 items.
could differentiate between hard/soft.

when using 6 feely boxes with a different object in each, could feel & describe
as either hard or soft, correctly.

Figure 5.1: Extract from 'Heather's' record

Tactile Display. (asked to touch & describe different materials) that's soft,
that's soft, that's soft . . . repeated this each time he touched a different
material. did this quickly, confidently & very enthusiastically. touched a sandal
& said "that's soft – no it's not, it's hard isn't it?" not waiting for an answer A.
cont. touching & saying "that's soft, etc." touched inside of biscuit pkt. said
"that's soft – look" turning to me showing he could push it down. A. touched
inside of choc-box (v. similar) could not push it down – said "that's hard – look"
showing me he couldn't push it down or squash it. He used this criteria for
determining whether material was soft or hard. Enjoyed this activity
tremendously. Kept returning to join in when other children were working with me.

Figure 5.2: Extract from 'Alex's' record

taneous play by a classroom assistant. From these observations Mo was able to
say that Heather is able to distinguish between hard and soft materials and is able
to talk about their similarities and differences. This was recorded as an example
of Heather's progress in her 'Knowledge and Understanding of the World'.

Mo made a longer record (Figure 5.2) of an important interaction with 'Alex' in
which he is showing through his actions that he is beginning to test the materials
in order to compare them. He had devised his own criteria for deciding whether a
material was hard or soft – he pushed down on the materials and, if he couldn't
squash it, decided that it was hard, if he could, it was soft. This spontaneous systematic approach to testing the materials showed some important attributes of scientific enquiry that could be encouraged and developed. This is a good example of
how, through observing his actions, Mo has been able to assess his development.

Making the records helps Mo to focus her observations and to identify what she
needs to plan for on a daily and weekly basis. This may take the form of particular activities or planning time to work with certain children in particular ways –
perhaps by 'modelling' how to make comparisons and ask scientific questions.
Other adults in the classroom are included in discussions about how to move each
child forwards. The records are also used in longer-term planning to inform

target-setting for the children and these targets are referred to in discussions with parents about how they might support children's learning at home.

As well as these formative assessments, Mo also maintains a summative record of each child's learning in which a date is recorded when the child demonstrates achievement against set criteria, e.g. 'Can use senses to explore materials'. This is useful in ensuring that a full range of learning and development is noted and where there are gaps in areas that have been the focus of assessment, these can be more easily identified.

Commentary

Mo's work demonstrates the power of observation as a formative assessment technique, leading to skilled and targeted interventions in learning. There are a number of other ways of gaining insight into young children's scientific skills and understanding, while providing a permanent record from which to plan.

Floorbooks

Essentially, a floorbook is a large format 'home-made' book of plain pages, made of 'sugar paper' or 'flip-chart' paper in which an adult or the children write and draw ideas, observations, predictions, questions and explanations. With young children the book is compiled on the floor so the group can all have a good view and opportunity to contribute. It can be completed during one session or revisited during a number of sessions. Floorbooks have a number of advantages as an assessment tool:

1. *They are motivational.* We know that learning is enhanced if we build on the existing ideas that children hold (Ollerenshaw and Ritchie 1997). We also know that in order for children to reveal their ideas they need to be situated in a non-threatening learning environment where their ideas are valued and accepted. The act of writing down what a child says, even if they cannot read it, provides a strong message to the child that what they say is important and, literally, note-worthy. It shows children that they can become actively involved in decision-making processes.
2. *They develop language skills and taking turns.* As children become used to this way of working they can begin to think how their ideas might be recorded in sentences, or as questions. They will have to take turns, listening to what others say before adding their own ideas.
3. *They provide opportunities for the teacher to model and share with children the writing process.* During the compilation of a floorbook the children will observe and may become curious about how their words are being transformed into writing. They will see the teacher using the conventions of writing.
4. *They can slow the conversation, allowing time for thought.* Recording children's ideas as they say them has its problems and requires some practice on the part of the teacher, but also requires the children to understand they need to wait. This

need not be a bad thing; children can have more time to think and develop and refine their ideas, or perhaps repeat them. We observed an example of this during the making of a film about science in the classroom: the director asked each child to repeat their contributions to a discussion so the camera operator could get a close-up of them in turn. In every case, the child had refined their ideas and made a clearer statement second time around.

5. *They record for assessment and evaluation.* Contributions can be initialled, or each child's ideas can be written in a different colour. The floorbook then provides a good record of the session that can be analysed and reflected upon. The information is likely to shed light on children's 'baseline' knowledge and understanding and also provide information about the effectiveness of the session. This can in turn lead to differentiation and inform evaluation respectively. During the session, criteria for evaluation and assessment may have been generated; for example, 'Have we answered the questions we started with?' might be a useful criterion. The case study below provides examples of this in practice.

Case study: A magnet floorbook

Angela Tipping, teaching at Bowsland Green Primary School in Bristol, had set up a display of magnets for the Reception class to explore in their first term at school. On one occasion she worked with groups of children to focus their attention on the display and assess their understanding.

Angela led the discussion and exploration while another adult made notes about the interactions in a floorbook, using a different coloured pen to record each child's ideas. In analysing the information afterwards it became apparent that children in the group had responded quite differently. For example, 'Louise' made a number of comments indicating the kinds of observations she was making during her exploration:

> 'The big magnets stick to each other.'
> 'They are wobbly [two "polo-mint" magnets on a dowel], they won't stick.'

From these and other comments it was clear that Louise was on her way to reaching the Early Learning Goals for exploration and investigation and would benefit from encouragement to find out about a wide range of things that interested her. 'Damien' made the following observations:

> 'When I stuck a magnet to another magnet they stuck really hard.'
> 'The can has metal on the back.'

Yet most of his utterances were questions:

> 'What happens when you spin [the magnet]?'
> 'What's under [the display] sticking to the magnet?'
> 'What happens when you slide them on each other?'

These indicated to Angela that Damien was achieving the following Early Learning Goal:

Ask questions about why things happen and how things work.

(QCA/DfEE 2000: 88)

She anticipated that he would benefit from support to be more systematic in his explorations in order to satisfy his curiosity.

'Ellie' made little comment during the session, although she was engrossed with the resources. Rather than make notes of what she said, the observer had sketched some examples of the ways in which Ellie had arranged the magnets – in 'trains' and 'ropes'. It was clear to Angela that she would need a lot of encouragement during the year to put her ideas in words and express them confidently in a group.

Commentary

Angela used the floorbook to elicit children's understanding about magnets and skills of scientific enquiry at the start of their time in school. Some schools have started to use a floorbook activity prior to planning for the next half-term unit. In this way plans can truly reflect the needs of the class and respond to what is in learners' minds.

Mind mapping

Mind mapping refers to a range of techniques for making visual representations of ideas and is closely associated with the development of thinking skills. In primary science, the most common form of mind map is the concept map (Novak and Gowin 1984), a formative assessment technique more appropriate to slightly older children than the floorbook – perhaps towards the end of Key Stage 1. In the process of constructing a concept map, learners are encouraged to think about how they see the connections between ideas and in the process to clarify their own thinking. The resulting map usually consists of words associated with a particular topic arranged across a page, with annotated arrows drawn to connect those that children see as linked, e.g.

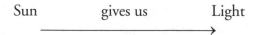

Teachers can use this process and the resulting maps to give them an insight into children's thinking and to identify where ideas may need to be challenged or developed. Concept maps can also be useful as way of helping children to be more aware of their own learning, particularly if they 'revisit' their maps at the end of a topic. There are ways of simplifying mind mapping that make it useful and productive with younger children (Ollerenshaw and Ritchie 1997) as illustrated in the case study below.

Case study: Mind mapping in Key Stage 1

Sue Hunt at Filton Hill Primary School in Bristol has developed the strategy of mind mapping to elicit children's scientific ideas in different ways in different year groups. In the examples below, Sue describes how she has carried out the elicitation strategies, the children's ideas that she selected as being particularly significant and the 'next steps' that she identified.

Year 1: Mapping cards

Activities where links are made between words can be carried out with very young children by using pictures on cards and scribing the children's responses. I made a set of cards with pictures and words linked to Year 1 work on plants. The cards were shared out between a group of ten children at the end of the topic. The children were each asked to find another child (or children) holding a card that they thought was linked to their card and be prepared to tell me why they were linked. Coloured lines represented the different groupings that the children formed as they made the links between the cards and the children's explanations for these groups were noted.

Two groups made links between structural parts of a plant (roots and stem, leaf, flower, plant). The next step from this was to question them further to see what they knew about the functions of the different parts of a plant and to develop these ideas. Another group had thought about seed dispersal:

'Seeds are from plants and they blow in the air.'

I decided to develop this in future lessons by asking why seeds are carried away from the parent plant. A fourth group put together factors necessary for healthy plant growth – water, sunlight and soil:

'Plants need these three to grow a lot – as their home and their food.'

This provided a starting point for investigative work to test these ideas.

Year 2: Mapping between two lists

We began with the heading 'Things that move' and the children came up with a list of suggestions. We then did the same for the next heading: 'How things move'. We then set about making links between the two columns of words (Figure 5.3). This activity was done at the beginning of the topic and showed me that the children already knew lots of the related vocabulary, establishing a starting point that was more advanced than I might have assumed without this elicitation.

Year 2: Extended brainstorms

I used whole-class brainstorming at the start of the next topic on living things (Figure 5.4). I then took it a stage further and asked children if they could think of other ideas linked to those already written down. For example, where one child

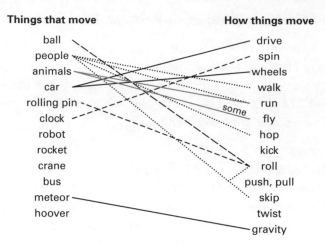

Figure 5.3: Mind mapping between two lists of words

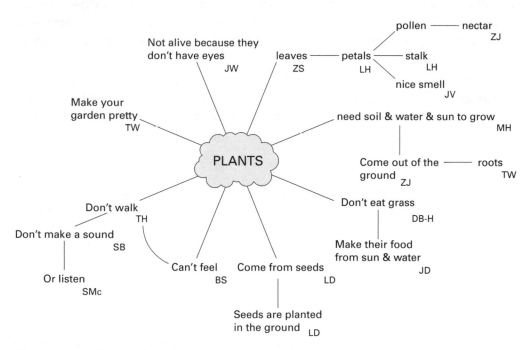

Figure 5.4: Example of an extended brainstorm

had contributed the idea that plants don't eat grass, another child made a link with the idea that they make their food from sun and water. This showed that the second child had some sophisticated ideas that could be discussed and developed further. To develop the idea that 'plants are not alive because they don't have eyes', I planned further work on the concept of 'alive' and 'not alive'.

At the end of the topic, children had a go at their own extended brainstorm. The girl who initially believed that plants are not alive demonstrated a change in ideas in her brainstorm by stating that 'plants need water, light, soil to keep alive'.

Another child made links between the different ways in which different animals are born:

'Some come out of eggs, some just come out of the bum [sic].'

This shows that he is seeing animals as a broader group than just mammals, but also raises an interesting alternative idea about reproduction to address!

Commentary

One of the issues that arise from this case study is that the children are clearly learning during the assessment; in constructivist terms *restructuring* (changing ideas) is taking place during *elicitation* (see Chapter 2). Questions posed by the teacher and ideas suggested by their peers led to discussions that may well have changed the children's thinking. It is important that assessment is not seen as a static process that is somehow separate from normal learning activities. The intention is not to produce a definitive list of things the child does and does not understand at any point in time, but to provide the teacher with insights into each child's thinking that may inform what happens in the next few minutes, as well as the next few weeks.

Concept cartoons

A further way of gaining access to learners' scientific ideas is to use an approach developed by Naylor and Keogh (1997; 2000) known as 'concept cartoons'. Each cartoon depicts an everyday science-based situation for children to think about, with three or four comments representing common 'alternative frameworks' written in speech bubbles from cartoon children. For example, in one cartoon three children are watching another child play with a toy car. Their three statements are:

(a) 'If I wind this car up twice as much it will go twice as far.'
(b) 'I think it will go twice as fast.'
(c) 'It won't make much difference.'

There are a number of ways in which this cartoon might be used: children could be asked as a class or group which character they agreed with (and why); they could indicate their preferred statement on a mini-whiteboard and discuss with a partner; or try the activity out. One strength of the technique is that children feel less anxious about exposing their own ideas as 'wrong' – the idea belongs to the character. It can also support children who find it difficult to express their own ideas in words; they can take the idea closest to their own thinking and work with it, evaluate and perhaps reject it. The ideas in the cartoons can be developed and made more meaningful to young children by acting them out with props and puppets taking on the roles.

Teachers often use a similar approach to gain access to children's thinking through role-play. By making obvious 'wrong', 'silly' or debatable statements, young children can be prompted into revealing their own understanding. Statements such as: 'Please get me my coat – I am really hot out here', or 'I think the batteries have run out of this push-along toy!' can prompt discussions that will generate assessment information.

Recording

The process of making records about children's progress and attainment can contribute significantly to the assessment process. The strategies for gathering formative assessment information discussed above provide some suggestions for recording systems that are an intrinsic part of the process of assessment. Strategies such as floorbooks and mind mapping provide a ready-made record. It is through analysing and discussing these and other sources of information that further light can be shed on children's understanding, how they learn best, and the best direction for future learning. Parents and all those that work with the child should contribute information. It is recommended by the QCA (2002) that for 3–5-year-olds this information is collated into a Foundation Stage Profile, which replaces baseline assessment from September 2002. The case study from Blaise Primary above demonstrates how Mo Pearson uses a combination of sources of evidence, including records of observations and conversations and annotated photographs of each child to keep an ongoing profile of their learning and development.

Reporting to parents and children

Most schools arrange structured meetings between teachers and parents during the year to discuss children's progress. However, Early Years practitioners are likely to have frequent, informal conversations with parents and carers about their children, and much informal reporting will take place this way. Conversations with parents should be seen as two-way processes of information sharing; opportunities should be created for parents to share their knowledge of the child in different contexts and this information added to the teacher's records.

There are general issues to be considered when reporting, such as the need for choosing language that is appropriate for the audience, but there are also issues that relate specifically to science and D&T. In both subjects the *processes* that children use are at least as important as the outcome, though this may not be immediately obvious to parents. For example, when shown an interesting glue and paper construction that a child has designed and made with little support, we may need to explain exactly what is impressive about the achievement – the creativity, the independence, the cutting skills and how it is a perfect fit as a cave for the plastic stegosaurus. In science and D&T, attitudes such as curiosity and willingness to try things out are important as well as developing concepts, but these may not be obvious achievements in the eyes of some parents. Indeed, our reports to parents may need to make the case for the inclusion of science and D&T in their children's learning, since their enquiries are unlikely to focus upon these areas.

Digital photographs are proving a powerful and versatile tool for teachers wanting to record the daily activity of the classroom. They could contribute to 'electronic' profiles with images, annotations and other records stored and available when reporting to parents. What could be more informative than showing parents images, even video clips of their children about their daily classroom business? An important and often neglected audience is the child themselves, as we have indicated by our focus on children's self-assessment in this chapter. Profiles with good visual content also enable children to review and reflect on their own progress.

Summary

We began this chapter by claiming that assessment is central to Early Years education, and that children's scientific and technological attitudes, skills and concepts should form part of what we assess. We have outlined the assessment requirements in Foundation Stage and Key Stage 1, providing guidance as to the broad content and criteria for our assessments. We have emphasised the primacy of assessment *for* learning, providing examples of a number of strategies for eliciting and recording science and D&T such as observation, floorbooks, mind mapping and concept cartoons. Finally, we have made the case for reporting to parents on their children's achievement in science and D&T, emphasising process over outcome.

CHAPTER 6

Science and D&T in the Foundation Stage

Alan Howe

Purpose of this chapter

Through reading this chapter you will gain

- an understanding of the Curriculum Guidance for the Foundation Stage in relation to science and D&T
- examples of how science and D&T can contribute to all the areas of learning in the Foundation Stage
- an understanding of the relationship between science and D&T in the Reception year and Key Stage 1.

Introduction: The fable of Donkey and Rabbit

Rabbit was very young and Donkey was very old and wise. Donkey knew why the sky was blue and why spiders don't stick to their webs. He wanted to teach Rabbit everything he knew. 'I can only teach you if you sit still and listen,' Donkey said to Rabbit. Donkey started telling Rabbit why the sky was blue. He looked up but Rabbit was off playing in the field. Next day Donkey tried again. As soon as he started, Rabbit was off chasing butterflies. Donkey got very cross. The next day, when again Rabbit went off to play, Donkey followed him. 'Do you know', said Rabbit, 'that some ladybirds have more spots than others?' Donkey didn't know that. 'I didn't know that,' he said, amazed. Donkey and Rabbit played together, counting flowers and watching bees. 'Didn't you want to tell me something?' said Rabbit. 'Never mind', said Donkey. 'It can wait.'

Developed from a story by Sally Grindley (Grindley and Varley 1996)

Nurturing attitudes to learning is perhaps the Early Years teacher's most important task. We know that most children begin school with lots of curiosity, enthusiasm, creativity and motivation. We have seen in previous chapters how a great deal of learning has happened before children step into the world of 'grant-funded' education. Children have experienced many scientific phenomena at home, outside, in the bath, or during mealtimes. They have begun to learn that they can modify their world according to their needs and wants. If the Foundation Stage is to build on these experiences, we must provide many more rich and varied encounters and begin the process of teaching children to become more aware, discerning and thoughtful about the natural and made world. This chapter describes how this might be achieved through science and D&T contexts.

Science and D&T in the Curriculum Guidance

Since its establishment in 2000 as a recognised phase in the curriculum for English schools, the Foundation Stage has become the crucial transition stage between early informal learning as described in Chapter 3 and the more formal expectations that are applied as children move into Key Stage 1. It is worth noting here that the Welsh Foundation Stage (3–7) maintains an informal focus for a longer time, which is in sympathy with the views of many Early Years educators. The *Curriculum Guidance for the Foundation Stage* (QCA/DfEE 2000) outlines key principles developed from the 'Rumbold Report' of 1990 (DES 1990), consultation within the sector and subsequent curriculum developments such as the 'Desirable Outcomes' (SCAA 1996). It is the 'core reference document for the successful implementation of the foundation stage' (foreword), showing how the key principles should be put into practice through teaching and attention to the diverse needs of children. The Curriculum Guidance is structured around areas of learning, since 'subjects' are not an appropriate basis for curriculum organisation in the Foundation Stage (see Chapter 1).

Science and D&T, however, *are* subjects in the National Curriculum, but they also represent fundamental ways of knowing about the world. This is why we think that it is so important that all children have access to them. It is often said, as a kind of shorthand, that 'science and D&T are *in* Knowledge and Understanding of the World'. This is a reference to the sentence in the Guidance which states that 'Knowledge and Understanding of the World forms the foundation for later work in science, design & technology, history, geography, and ICT' (QCA/DfEE 2000: 82). However, in my view there is not quite such a straightforward correlation between 'subjects' and 'areas of learning'. For example, science and D&T are both subjects that develop and require creativity (NACCCE 1999; Howe *et al.* 2001), yet we are told in the Guidance that the area of 'Creative Development' includes only 'art, music, dance, role-play and imaginative play'.

Nicholls (1999) argues that young pupils' scientific work should not be constrained by a rigid curriculum framework, but should be prompted from natural curiosity. It is difficult to predict the focus of children's curiosity; if we are to be able to respond to it then a flexible 'framework' is required. De Boo (2000: 2–3) identifies the tension between the nature of early learning and the requirement to use time in a structured way:

As the infant grows there is more to learn and less time in which to learn it, less time for the countless repetitions of infancy . . . In nurseries or early years class-rooms, time has to be structured so as to give children the maximum experience of familiar and unfamiliar phenomena in as short a time as possible, whilst still allowing enough repetitive play to convince them and enable them to make reasonable generalisations . . . if we are successful in helping children to be confident explorers, aware of their own scientific skills, how to apply them more consistently and economically (time-wise) . . . we will have equipped them for lifelong learning.

In their analysis of the Curriculum Guidance, Siraj-Blatchford and Siraj-Blatchford (2001) find that it does indeed support the idea that practitioners should make effective use of unexpected and unforeseen opportunities for children's learning and that there is a general acceptance in the document of the appropriateness of 'emergent' learning. The Curriculum Guidance does not state *which* specific scientific or technological knowledge is to be gained during the Foundation Stage. Many of the skills identified across the areas of learning are, however, science and D&T-related, as we shall see through the case studies below.

Case study: Personal, social and emotional development

Many of the children in the Reception class of trainee-teacher John Paul Sharman had very little direct experience of animals. With the support of his teacher-mentor, John Paul planned a range of activities to introduce children to a range of animals. He was careful to check school policies, LEA guidance and legal issues before beginning. He sent a letter to all parents asking for information regarding children's known allergies. He was also careful to find out whether animal bedding or feed (for example those containing nuts) might cause allergic reaction. At the same time he asked parents if they could help in any way with the topic of 'animals'.

The topic began gently with 'James' bringing in his rabbit from home. James was able to talk to the class about how he cared for the pet, its need for exercise, handling (to keep it good-natured) and feeding. In this way the class began to think about the needs of living things. When another pet made a visit to school, 4½-year-old 'Kim' astounded the class and the teacher by demonstrating her expertise in the care of poodles, since her mother was a dog-breeder. She explained to her peers how she 'groomed' the poodles by shampooing, 'clipping around the muzzle' and brushing their coats.

For two weeks the class hosted a colony of African land snails. The children were taught how to care for these amazing molluscs – they need regular spraying with water-mist and enjoy a diet of fresh cucumber. Because the snails are very large, the children could clearly see the way they 'rasped' their way through the cucumber and how they moved on ripples of their 'foot' as they travelled up the glass side of their tank. The children made links to other experiences with snails

and slugs, realising why their parents needed to keep them away from their precious garden plants.

The death of animals was a significant part of the project. One child was hoping
to bring his pet dog in to share with the class, but it fell ill and died during the
term. Children discussed such losses openly; they shared experiences about
burying dead pets and where they had 'gone', although John Paul noticed children often talked about dead pets in the present tense and seemed to think a
replacement pet was the original pet in a new guise. He felt the discussions helped
children begin to understand death and bereavement.

The next visitor to school was a horse, although John Paul kept clear due to an
allergy. Discussions about the care for this animal provided a good opportunity
for the children to think about similarities and differences; both the horse and the
snails enjoyed apples, while the differences were easier to identify. An education
officer, Vicki Thomas, from the Royal Society for the Prevention of Cruelty to
Animals (RSPCA), was the next visitor to the class. She did not bring any animals
with her, as the RSPCA have a policy of advising teachers not to keep animals in
school. During the workshop she encouraged them to think about the needs that
all pets have: food, clean water, exercise, a safe and comfortable place to live and
sleep, grooming to keep them healthy and 'love' (i.e. freedom from injury, fear and
stress, and the opportunity to behave naturally) for all their lives. The teacher used
this framework of six needs in future weeks when the children encountered other
more unusual creatures. Having a visitor in class also gave the children opportunity to practise listening, raising questions and responding to a different adult in
a change of routine – all aspects of 'stepping stones' to Early Learning Goals in
this area. Social development also featured in a trip to Bristol Zoo; again children
were having to adapt to a new situation in a different environment. At the zoo the
education officer was rather taken aback by the level of knowledge the children
already had about the care of animals. For example, the children were shown a
cage with a rat inside but otherwise empty. They were able quickly to identify what
the zoo should provide in order to care for it properly. The children were then
introduced to a python and some hissing cockroaches. They heard about the need
for animals to have appropriate and varied diets and careful handling (e.g. always
to stroke a python with the back of the hand to avoid transferring sweat and salts
to its skin) before seeing the rest of the zoo.

John Paul concluded the topic with an 'empathy session'. Children took it in
turns to be an animal. The others then asked the child how they would feel if they
were hit, or mistreated, or not fed. This helped the children think back to all they
had learned about caring for animals and apply it to this situation.

Commentary

This delightful case study shows how, with a considerable amount of planning and
thought; children's scientific experiences of living things can be enriched enormously during the Foundation Stage. The work described above addressed many of

the stepping stones toward the ELGs for personal, social and emotional development, including those related to dispositions and attitudes, behaviour, self-control and self-care. It also shows that the local community and the children themselves can contribute towards this learning. John Paul acknowledges that the topic would not have been half as successful without the parents' support.

Case study: Knowledge and understanding of the world

It is early November in the Reception class at St Philip's Primary in Bath. The children have settled into school and baseline assessments have been completed. The teacher has decided to introduce some new scientific experiences. With intentions based on the Early Learning Goal of 'investigating objects and materials by using all the senses', Alison the class teacher introduces the afternoon's activities by referring to prior experiences the children have recently shared:

> Alison: *We have done a lot of listening, and talking recently, to find out about things. How else do we find out about things?*
> *Let's say we are walking along and hear a noise . . . how could we find out more?*
> Child: *Ask a teacher.*
> Alison: *How else?*
> Child: *Wait for someone to come along?*

This is not going to be easy. Alison was hoping to open a discussion about observation, and how we might use all our senses to explore the world about us. She tries another tack and puts a teddy into the middle of the carpet.

> Alison: *How can I found out about him?*
> Child: *Pick him up.*
> Alison: *(picks bear up) He's furry! I can feel him. How else can I find out about him?*
> Child: *Look at him!*

This first discussion of observational skills is now under way. The children talk about what they can see, and what they can tell from looking: for example, 'The floor's shiny,' 'The carpet's furry.' The idea of 'viewing' the world through a cardboard kitchen roll inner is introduced. The children are keen to have a go. It has the effect of focusing their attention to specific objects: 'We're like pirates looking out for ships.' In the final part of the introduction Alison introduces the idea of putting coloured cellophane filters over the viewers (Figure 6.1).

Alison explains: 'I am going to make Jack look different, but I'm not going to touch him. Look! He's gone red!' The children's curiosity is now stimulated. They all want to try this new game. Adults show groups how to make the viewers and they freely explore with the three coloured filters available. Some children notice that things look all red, or brighter, or different. Alison notes this; the activity has shown that some children are ready to be moved on by closer questioning. Many

Figure 6.1: Looking through coloured cellophane

children have difficulty articulating their observations and many deny what they can see. To the adults in the room it is obvious that the colours of the learning support assistant's rugby shirt or of the display boards appear to change, yet the children can only say that everything looks the colour of the filter, or insist that the colours do not change.

The afternoon session breaks into a variety of activities. One group explores a box of torches, filters and mirrors. They enjoy looking in a big convex mirror (Figure 6.2); at one time they are upside-down, the next the right way up. A boy hides behind a chair and peeps over with a periscope; a kaleidoscope captivates another. One girl has two torches and chases the beams across the floor and ceiling. The adult with them shows her they can be reflected back, but she is not interested in that. All the children are quite happy to explore the collection of new things. Knowledge has been developed: knowledge of mirrors, filters, torches and colours. There is no telling whether the new experience will be stored and saved, but it will certainly contribute to children's greater understanding of the world.

The session is recorded using a digital camera. After afternoon play the photographs are shared with the children as they gather around the computer screen. They recognise themselves and their friends engaged in the activities. They are encouraged to note that the camera too has experienced the same effects as their

Figure 6.2: Looking in a convex mirror

eyes – boys have turned red, the room has gone yellow. The images are saved to illustrate a planned class book on this new experience.

Commentary

This case study shows children not only gaining knowledge but also developing their observational skills. Observing and naming colours is a common theme in Early Years settings, yet here children are presented with a concept – that filters can change the apparent colour of an object – that is not easily assimilated within their existing understanding of colour. For some, this leads them to reject the evidence of their eyes; they are reluctant to 'unlearn' what they have so recently learned. Yellow cannot suddenly become green, or red become black. The phenomenon is similar to that which occurs when children, when asked to make an 'observational drawing', draw what they know about such an object – a flower or a toy – rather than what they can really see before them. Perhaps for these children the leap in understanding required for them to assimilate this new idea was beyond their Zone of Proximal Development (Vygotsky 1962). The children had not yet learned to observe closely, so reverted to internal, schematic representations that they had developed to help them make sense of colour. It is through carefully selected experiences – ones that may seem to contradict children's current understanding – that scientific understanding is often developed. Johnston (1996: 60) believes that 'providing different ways to package science ideas' can help motivate children and encourage them to think about the science involved. She suggests a number of 'tricks' that may fascinate children and prompt them to offer an explanation. I know my own children have been fascinated by my endless 'magic tricks' such as dropping a satsuma, balanced on top of a football, at the same time, or putting bicarbonate of soda and vinegar in a 'film pot' and closing the lid (stand well back in both cases!). Johnston warns, however, that, as in the case study above, 'fun' activities must have at their heart specific learning intentions in order to ensure such entertainment is underpinned by a clear idea of how the experiences will contribute to children's learning.

Communication, language and literacy

We have seen in Chapter 4 the close relationship that exists between language and learning in science and D&T. That chapter covers much of the ground in relation to this area of learning, so I do not intend to add significantly to it here. Table 6.1 shows how the Curriculum Guidance offered in terms of 'effective teaching requirements' for communication, language and literacy (QCA/DfEE 2000: 46) might be fulfilled through science and D&T contexts. This table could be used to audit practice in Early Years settings in order to judge whether children are having sufficient access to language that is specific to science and D&T.

Case study: Healthy eating and mathematical development

An example from the teaching of Louise Hern, a trainee teacher in her final teaching experience at Newbridge St John's Infant School, Bath, shows how a scientific context can provide opportunities for mathematical development. In her Reception class of 25 children she had planned a range of activities around a 'health' theme. To begin the topic the children had discussed their experiences of hospitals and doctors; had discussed what it meant to be 'healthy' and how one keeps healthy; received visits from health professionals and listened to stories about doctors. By week 3 of this topic, the children had gained a lot of knowledge about their own health and Louise drew this from them through discussion and questioning.

The children had a range of ideas about how hygiene, diet and exercise contributed to health. During one afternoon of this third week the children were asked to think about snacks: what they are, when we eat them, which ones we prefer. In the classroom they were given the chance to taste five different snacks: an apple, flapjack, crisps, toffees and raisins.

There was a great deal of interest as each group of 5 or 6 children took their turn to work with Louise to discuss and identify their favourite snack. The children's preferences were then recorded on a chart as a pictogram, with children drawing their favourite on stickers that were then placed in columns. When all the class had recorded their preferences children were eager to discuss the findings.

Table 6.1: Developing communication, language and literacy goals in science and design & technology contexts

Effective teaching requirement	Example from science and design & technology contexts
Practitioners valuing talk and alternative forms of communication	Encourage children to share memories and observations about the natural and 'manmade' world through listening actively to children's observations, thoughts and memories. Encourage talk and gesture to explain to others how a construction kit was used to make a model, or play led to a new discovery about the properties of a material.
Practitioners observing children and planning for the contexts in which they best develop their speaking and listening and their understanding of reading and writing	Make the most of opportunities when children bring found objects, toys or other items with scientific or design and technology potential. Ensure that on occasion, topics and themes chosen can lead to the introduction of new scientific and technical vocabulary and that there is access and reference to written material – books, websites, posters, packaging, etc. – with scientific and technological content.
Practitioners demonstrating the use of language for reading and writing	Through the use of floorbooks or other shared writing (see Chapter 5) practitioners can model scientific writing as they record children's observations about a collection of objects, or on observations the children have made about seasonal changes outside, changes in materials, similarities and differences of artefacts.
Practitioners modelling the use of language as a tool for thinking	Model scientific and technological language by talking out loud – 'I wonder what would happen if?', 'I think what will happen is . . .', 'I think I need to do this first . . .', 'If I put that piece there, then . . .', 'I didn't notice that before . . .'
Practitioners helping children to develop language for communication through interaction and expression	Encourage children to report on what they have done – 'How did you do that?', 'Can you tell us what you found out/saw/did?' Introduce appropriate language and encourage children to try it out – 'We have discovered . . . we predict . . . we have designed . . . we have constructed.' Encourage children to use, or even sing, comparative language – 'The cold chocolate is harder, the warm chocolate is softer . . . cold is harder . . . warm is softer.'

Table 6.1: (*cont.*)

Effective teaching requirement	Example from science and design & technology contexts
Practitioners helping children understand how text works	Ensure non-fiction and fiction books on scientific and technological topics (see Chapter 10) are available and shared with the class. Discuss how books and the internet can be used to answer questions and find new things out.
Planning that is flexible and informed and that involves the whole team	See Chapter 7 – Planning

Louise asked: 'Can you tell, just by looking at the pictogram, which snack is most people's favourite?' Many of the children were able to identify that toffees were the most popular (in spite of all the work about dentists and health) because:

> *'More people have drawn toffees on their stickers.'*
> *'You had to make the paper bigger because toffees went off the page.'*

When asked how this idea could be checked, someone suggested counting the stickers and writing the totals under each column. The children were asked, 'Does it still tell us that most people liked toffees best?' The class agreed that it did 'because it's a bigger number than the crisps'.

Commentary

This cameo of a typical, busy afternoon in a Reception class shows how a scientific context of health care and an enquiry supported by the class teacher can provide a meaningful context for mathematical development. Contexts take time to develop; it is rather like 'setting the scene' in a film or play. Once the scene is set, then activities will seem more motivating, relevant and mutually supporting. The above is an example of data handling, which will be developed through children's primary education in maths and ICT, yet is often applied in science contexts. It is therefore important that even at an early age, children learn to appreciate the close connection that exists between mathematics and science, and they become familiar with using mathematical language to express their developing scientific understanding. For children to be able to make a comparison ('this plant in the light was taller than the one in the dark'), order a sequence ('we saw lots of trees, quite a few flies and a few spiders'), identify a fair test ('we put the same amount of water in both containers'), mathematical understanding and vocabulary are required. *The National Numeracy Strategy* (DfEE 1999: 17) is very clear about this relationship: 'Almost every scientific investigation or experiment is likely to require one or more of the mathematical skills of classifying, counting, measuring, calculating, estimating, and recording in tables and graphs.' In D&T, work with textiles, card, paper, mouldable materials and construction kits all offer real contexts for measuring, counting, sorting and calculating. As they play with these materials and begin to make new products with them they will learn about faces, corners, vertices, angles, regular and irregular shapes long before they learn the correct terminology for these features.

Physical development

Physical development 'is about *improving skills* . . . it helps children gain confidence in what they can do and enables them to feel the positive benefits of being *healthy* and *active*' (my italics) (QCA/DfEE 2000: 100). There are two principal areas to consider here:

The development of *physical skills* can be considered on the 'fine-motor' and 'gross-motor' levels. Science and D&T contexts offer considerable scope for the development of both. When children are 'playing the scientist game' (Chapter 9) they will be taught to use special equipment such as magnifying glasses, 'bug boxes', 'pooters' (a tool for collecting insects and the like), liquid droppers and cameras. When making things children will improve their dexterity and learn new skills, such as cutting, joining, mixing, cooking and constructing (see Chapter 10).

The case study above shows children developing some of the physical skills associated with *keeping healthy*, working towards the Physical Development ELG of 'recognising the importance of keeping healthy and those things that contribute to it' (QCA/DfEE 2000: 110). The health of the nation is currently of national concern, and a government priority is to prevent future problems through promoting a healthy and balanced diet. A major strand of this strategy involves education, with initiatives such as the 'eat five-a-day' campaign and the National Healthy School Standard (NHSS). An evaluation of the National School Fruit Scheme (NSFS, due to be fully implemented by 2004), whereby all infant children will be provided with a piece of fruit a day, also supports the integration of 'healthy messages' into the school curriculum through scientific contexts. D&T, in the form of food technology activities, can help children to prepare and combine foods in a safe and healthy way, while providing a further context for informal conversations about diet, health and hygiene.

Being active

Stevens (2002) outlines a number of activities for children to do on a windy day which will encourage gross motor skills and full-body activity. She suggests that a 'windy day box' might include assorted streamers, windmills, balloons and pumps. Table 6.2 provides some additional ideas for 'weather boxes' that will encourage physical activity whatever the weather. The Curriculum Guidance has a number of references to children working outdoors. It is suggested that practitioners 'make good use of outdoor space so that children are enabled to learn by working on a

Table 6.2: Weather boxes

Sunny day activities	Windy day activities
Chalk drawing around shadows	Washing line and pegs
Following shadows as they move across the classroom or playground during the day	Streamers made from cellophane, textiles, paper and wool
Painting with water and brushes on the patio	Windsocks and 'windbags'
Putting things out to dry – washing, paintings, wet sand	Windmills
A collection of sunglasses and sun hats to dress up in	Balloons and pumps
Umbrellas and parasols	Parachuted toys
Making hats	Kites
A collection of transparent, opaque and translucent shapes to experiment with	
Bubble mixture	
NB: never allow children to look at the sun	

Rainy day activities	Cold, icy and snowy day activities
Chalk for drawing around puddles	Scrapers to scrape the ice
Wipeable pens to trace raindrops on windows	Black paper cones to catch flakes
Raincatchers and trays	Containers to collect ice and snow
Talc or powder paint to sprinkle in puddles	A collection of odd gloves to try out
Umbrellas	Objects to make tracks in snow – follow the tracks
Absorbent paper tongues for 'licking-up' puddles	
Boats to float	

larger, more active scale than is possible indoors' (QCA/DfEE 2000: 15). This can be ensured by planning in a regular time when children are taken outside to explore an aspect of the environment; often it will be a 'welly walk', but bad weather should be no excuse. As the Norwegians allegedly say, 'There is no such thing as bad weather, only bad clothes.'

Creative development

Early Years educators were heartened to find 'creative development' appearing in the *Desirable Outcomes for Children's Learning* (SCAA 1996) and retained in the Early Learning Goals of 2000, though its definition appears rather restricted. The government report *All Our Futures* (NACCCE 1999: 27) is very clear that creativity should not only be associated with the arts: 'creativity is not unique to the arts. It is equally fundamental to advances in the sciences, in mathematics, technology, in politics, business and in all areas of everyday life.' Those working with young children will have no difficulty in accepting the premise that all the children in their charge have the potential for creativity throughout the curriculum, for we witness children's creativity on a daily basis. Harrington (1990) brings the factors of process, people and physical environment together within a theoretical framework of the 'Creative Ecosystem'. Just as a balanced biological ecosystem can sustain life, so a creative ecosystem could be said to sustain creative output. The creative ecosystem in Early Years settings will have two key components: access to appropriate resources and spaces, and adults that understand and can support children's creativity.

Resources and spaces

Play is closely associated with creativity (Howe *et al.* 2001; Claxton 1998; Robinson 2001). Designers are very good at 'playing around' with ideas and materials (see Chapter 2), and while they do this new ideas and ways of working come to mind. Much of children's creativity will begin with an interaction with resources and spaces. Sand, water, construction kits, recycled materials, bits and pieces of all shapes and sizes will elicit creative activity. By providing new resources children can be encouraged to play in a new way and find out new things about the world. We have seen in relation to 'physical development' above how playing with resources can support children's learning about the outdoor environment. Indoors, sand and water trays are standard equipment in Early Years settings and offer a great deal of potential for play and creativity. Water can be warm, cold, icy, frozen, bubbly, coloured or perfumed while sand can be supplemented with a wide range of tools and toys or replaced by other materials such as leaves or compost. Art materials lend themselves to a number of scientific explorations. Working with clay can lead children to discoveries about reversible and irreversible change; wax resist techniques (e.g. painting with cooking oil and powder colour wash) can reveal that oil and water will not mix; drawing and painting on different surfaces and papers can demonstrate absorbency properties. Providing resources on their own, however, is not enough; there is another vital ingredient to consider: the adult.

Adults' role in supporting creative development

To be creative children need support to see further potential in the familiar (Howe *et al.* 2001). Children also need 'permission' to take risks. Being creative is a risky business which can end in tears; an unsatisfactory model that falls apart, lots of mess to clear up, lots of waste, unkind comments from peers are all potential outcomes of a creative endeavour. Children may already have had enough of being creative if it means they get into trouble! The adult's role here is to help children through the tricky tasks of planning what to do; knowing where to find and use resources, how to reconcile problems. Creativity does not therefore happen in an atmosphere of 'non-intervention'; rather it happens as knowledge and skills are applied. Getting these interventions 'right' is the subject of Chapters 9 and 10.

Involving children in decision-making

Children can have an input to the decisions we make about how things could be and should be in their learning environment. When setting up a classroom, re-arranging, sorting or labelling resources, children's ideas and needs and wants can be sought and discussed. Most classrooms have a role-play area that changes use from time to time. Involving children in setting up this area provides a genuine context for creative thinking, planning and action as they decide with their teacher what the new space might become and how it might be organised. For example, a Nursery teacher, Debbie Bateman at Hawksley Primary School, Birmingham, has set up with her class a beautiful sensory space.

Case study: Setting up a 'sensory space'

Debbie needed to be clear about the aims of the sensory room project before convincing the head teacher that it would be good use of valuable classroom space. These aims were:

- *to create an environment that stimulates the children's imagination by appealing to their senses*
- *to encourage active, hands-on investigation of the environment using touch, sight, smell and listening skills*
- *to create an environment that calms the children or lifts their confidence, depending on the lighting*
- *to develop auditory, visual and kinaesthetic learning skills*
- *to provide a room that transports the children from the present into a 'fantasy environment' to fire their imagination on a journey into the unknown.*

In response to these aims, the head teacher acted as 'permission giver' – an important role in facilitating creativity in teachers as well as children. Children and their parents were involved as much as possible. Some items were donated – such as fibre optic lights and hanging mobiles, while the school purchased a 'light table' specifically designed for young children to work at, by selecting, sorting and arranging transparent, translucent and opaque materials. Children were involved in the decision-making required: Where should things go? What theme should the room have? How should the room be used? and so on. The teacher noted that the children have subsequently shown more confidence in making choices about their environment.

The room has a theme that changes from time to time. This provides a focus from which the children design artefacts and create artwork to hang from the ceiling and cover walls and floor. Thus far the room has been the surface of the moon, a rainforest jungle and a circus. When in tranquil mode, it has a very calming effect on children and staff. They enjoy sitting quietly and watching the changes in colour on the various fibre optic, 'bubble' and 'disco' lights and listening to a range of music and sounds.

Commentary

As well as stimulating creative development, staff have noticed children's imaginative talk and play developing dramatically in response to the themes, together with motivation to investigate the objects on the light table; beginning to ask questions such as 'What if . . . ? How does it work?' They also co-operate and play well together in the space and are keen to share their experiences and discoveries with others.

Summary

In this chapter we have identified how science and design & technology can offer ideal contexts for the development of skills, attitudes, knowledge and understanding right across the early learning goals. We have seen how practitioners working from the Curriculum Guidance for the Foundation Stage have used such contexts in a number of settings to ensure children have rich and varied experiences which develop appropriate mathematical, communication, personal and social skills and support physical and creative development alongside the acquisition of knowledge and understanding of the world. In Chapters 9 and 10 we will describe how this rich holistic learning can be developed through Key Stage 1.

CHAPTER 7

Planning for science and D&T in the Foundation Stage

Tonie Scott and Sandy Sheppard

Purpose of this chapter

Through reading this chapter you will gain

- understanding of how to structure the Foundation Stage learning environment for science and D&T
- examples of long-, medium- and short-term planning for the Foundation Stage with science and D&T in mind.

Introduction

> Good planning is the key to making children's learning effective, exciting, varied and progressive . . . the process works best when all practitioners working in the setting are involved.
>
> (QCA 2001: 2)

We are Foundation Stage teachers (one Nursery, one Reception) at a primary school in Somerset which is attended by 190 children aged between 3 and 11. This chapter contains a rationale and description of our planning for science and D&T in the Foundation Stage which we hope you will find useful when developing plans for your own setting. It is always a challenge to meet the varying needs of individual children and to deliver all the required elements of the curriculum. We have found that it is necessary to establish a framework of intended learning, and then to be flexible; adapting and adjusting plans as the need arises. Planning across the Foundation Stage is shared between staff to ensure that children build upon previous experience.

Our broad aims for the Foundation Stage in our school are to provide

- a positive atmosphere in which children feel secure and valued
- a curriculum in which children are empowered to develop confidence and independence

- opportunities to learn through play
- a rich environment in which children develop a positive attitude to learning.

Our model for planning has evolved over several years and is continually being reviewed and updated. It is an example of one planning approach and is not intended to be prescriptive. For further examples see the QCA document *Planning for Learning in the Foundation Stage* (QCA 2001).

Long-term planning

We consider the main aspects of long-term planning to be:

- The establishment of clear ethos and aims for areas of learning.
- The provision of an appropriate physical environment, both indoors and outdoors.
- Plans to ensure progression, breadth of experience, and coverage of the statutory curriculum.

Aims for science and D&T within long-term planning

We feel that it is essential for children to be active participants in their learning and to be given the freedom to explore their own ideas and choices. We believe that this freedom helps to promote enquiry and creativity, which lays the foundations for successful learning in science and D&T.

When planning we are careful to consider appropriate experiences and the provision of sufficient support for the development of attitudes, skills and knowledge that will lay the foundations for learning in science and D&T. We try to create an environment that fosters enquiry and develops children's confidence as creators while encouraging attitudes of curiosity, confidence, perseverance, independence, open-mindedness and co-operation which will enable children to become more successful learners. We also aim to develop scientific and design and technological knowledge in a way that is integrated with the learning of new skills.

In order to achieve these aims we see three elements to balance in long-term planning: *teacher-directed tasks*, *directed play activities* and *free play activities*. It is essential to ensure that there is a balance of tasks, activities and experiences throughout the year. It is also necessary to plan for progression across the Foundation Stage and into Key Stage 1. With our aims in mind, our long-term plan (Table 7.1) demonstrates how we identify activities against the Early Learning Goals and set them in familiar and relevant contexts, or 'topics'. We plan topics or themes to draw different aspects of the curriculum together. The use of topics can

- help to place science and D&T in a meaningful context
- provide a useful starting point from which the children's interests and ideas can flow
- provide opportunities for parents and carers to become involved
- enable focused work on particular areas of learning for a few weeks at a time – this gives the opportunity to teach specific science or design & technology skills.

Table 7.1: Example of long-term planning in the Foundation Stage

Term: Autumn	Topic: Colour and shape	Topic: Post Office
Role play	Home corner	Post Office
		Deliver cards at Christmas time
Personal, social and emotional development (PSED)	Settling in to school routines	Favourite presents
	Meet 'buddies'	Class book about giving and sharing
	Planning boards	Ourselves, families and friends
	Ring games & circle time (C. time)	Christmas stories
Communication, language and literacy (CLL)	Colour stories and poems	Listening walk, listening games
	Elmer stories	Write – letters, invitations, lists
	Big Book stories – Hungry Giant, Mrs Wishy Washy	Introduce author – Mick Inkpen
	Taking books home to read	Use picture dictionaries for initial sounds
	Name and writing pattern every day	The Jolly Postman story
	Introduce language area, for example in literacy sessions	Writing table
		Introduce Oxford Reading Tree
Mathematical development (MD)	Repeating patterns	Weigh parcels – heavy and light – language
	Introduce Maths area	Sort parcels and presents
	2-D shapes	Count and sort letters
	Number recognition	Sort 3-D shapes
	Colour graph	
	Straight and curved lines and shapes	
	Number songs and rhymes	
Knowledge and understanding of the world (KUW)	Colour in nature	Autumn and seasons
	Make biscuits	Sort wrapping papers
	Sort leaves, bulbs, conkers, etc.	Explore sound, make instruments
	Explore the school	Christmas in the past
	Animal colours and camouflage environment	Make truffles
	Explore coloured filters, prisms, light	
	Design a home to hide an animal	

Table 7.1: (*cont.*)

Term: Autumn	Topic: Colour and shape	Topic: Post Office
ICT	Dazzle	Roamer
	Animated Alphabet	Animated Numbers
		Pendown
		Dazzle
Physical development (PD)	Use of space in the hall	Use range of balls and equipment
	Moving around safely	Simple games
	Explore large apparatus	Footwork – fast and slow
	Footwork	Autumn dance
Creative development (CD)	Fruit printing	Colour mixing
	Colour mixing	Nelson music – percussion
	Story chest songs	Explore inks, oil pastels
	Collage	Weaving
	Action songs, finger rhymes	Christmas songs and performance

To achieve our long-term plans we need to:

• provide a wide range of interesting and stimulating resources
• provide adult support for planned and unplanned activities
• respond to children's interests, interacting with them and discussing materials, objects and events
• encourage children to observe, explore and experiment
• work as a team ensuring that all adults working with children contribute to the ethos and aims of the learning environment.

Planning the physical environment

The physical environment needs to be organised in a way that enhances opportunities for learning. We try to create an environment that is interesting and attractive, caters for the needs of the children and enables us to deliver the curriculum. The learning environment is planned so that resources are easily accessible, to enable children to select and store them independently. There are also clearly designated areas for different types of activity, for example, construction, puzzles, collage.

English, science, mathematics and D&T resources have colour-coded labels. This encourages children to locate independently the equipment they need. For example, magnifying glasses will always be in one of the red drawers. It is a strategy that

Table 7.2: Planning the physical environment: materials for exploration, designing and making in the nursery

Sand	Water	Malleable materials
Dry sand/wet sand	Recycled materials	*Playdough with:*
Recycled materials	Boats and people	Rolling pins and cutters
Dry sand and wheels	Water wheels	Textured rollers
Dinosaurs	Funnels and pipes	Syringes
Vehicles	Funnels, jugs and bottles	Moulds
Bottles and jugs	Coloured water	Plastic numbers/letters
Stacking beakers	Bubbles, pipes and blowers	Scales
Spoons and scoops	Toy animals	Tea set
Buckets and spades	Popoids, stickle bricks, etc.	Plates and cutlery
Sieves	Tea set	Small sticks
Duplo	Water clocks	Straws
Small wooden bricks	Foam numbers and letters	Plastic scissors and knives
Sticks and leaves	Containers with holes	
Animals	Pipes and gutters, etc.	
Sand moulds	Washing dolls	Different types of dough, for example salt dough, stretchy dough
Sieves and treasure	Floating and sinking	
Tiny things	Shells	
	Squirty bottles and water pistols	
Alternative materials:		
Compost	Clear tray over colourful paper with shiny objects	Clay
Lentils		Plasticine
Rice	Saucepans and wooden spoons with coloured water	Cornflour and water
Leaves		
	Washing clothes	
	Ice	

enables us to plan resources with progression in mind, for example, construction kits become progressively more challenging.

We are fortunate that the nursery is purpose built and a spacious area, so it is possible for resources to be openly displayed and clearly visible. The children can see what is available and make choices about where they want to play and what equipment they would like to use. The Reception and Key Stage 1 classes are much

Figure 7.1: Investigating reflective objects in outdoor water play

smaller, and many resources are stored in drawers, all at the children's level. To enable the children to select their activities, each area has a planning board displaying photographs of available resources. These photos may be changed if there is a particular focus, for example a collection of moving toys becomes one of the options when forces are part of our topic work.

We vary the equipment available in each area to ensure that the learning environment provides a range of experiences to stimulate the children's interest and encourage exploration and enquiry. Table 7.2 lists some of the resources we use to support children's exploration and the beginnings of designing and making.

Using the outdoor environment

We make extensive use of the outdoor environment. It is a wonderful resource for science activities such as investigating natural materials, gardening and water play (Figure 7.1). Space for larger construction tasks enables children to design, build and change their own structures and engage in imaginative play, thus creating their own meaningful context. Construction kits such as Quadro and big bricks are very useful; however, resources for these activities do not need to be expensive. Sizeable pieces of fabric can be used as blankets, picnic rugs or to make dens. Milk crates may be available from a local dairy; these are light, versatile and function as very large bricks that fit together to make houses, barriers and enclosures.

The children used the milk crates to make an aeroplane in the nursery garden. Every day they arrived at nursery, made an aeroplane and 'flew' to a different

Figure 7.2: Outside construction using milk crates

country. Each day the aeroplane was slightly larger and more intricate as more children became involved (Figure 7.2). The game evolved to include looking for wild animals, particularly lions. One of the children had seen the lions at Longleat Safari Park and described this experience to the class. Another child knew that there were lions in Africa. Using a site with a web cam on the internet, the children were able to watch lions and other animals visiting a waterhole in Africa. A visit was then organised to see the lions at Longleat.

We also go for walks around the school grounds and local community. Walks outdoors have a clear purpose, often linked to the science areas currently being explored. If the children have a focus it helps them to concentrate, and to reflect afterwards on what has been experienced and discovered. Outdoor walks can also lead to other areas for exploration.

The nursery class were on a 'listening walk' in the school grounds. There had been a storm during the previous night and a large branch had been blown from one of the trees. The children examined the branch for a while, and then Matthew asked, 'Can we take it back to the nursery?' Kerry became enthusiastic and said, 'Yeah, then we can cut it up with the saw!' This led to a lot of discussion about health and safety, the weight of the branch, and which children would be strong enough to carry it. Over the next few days the children took turns to use the saw to cut pieces of wood from the branch. They were very pleased with themselves and took their wood home to show their parents.

One recent development, which has worked well at our school, is the involvement of the Year 6 children. Each child in the Reception class is allocated a 'buddy' to offer support during their first year at school. When the Year 6 class accompany their buddies for outdoor science activities, they help the younger children to focus and talk about their discoveries. They can also give help with recording the activity.

Medium-term planning

We consider the main aspect of medium-term planning to be adapting the broad and general framework of long-term plans to meet the specific needs of the children. This entails

- Using our prior knowledge and formative assessment of the children to plan exciting activities, taking into account their needs and interests.
- Identifying learning objectives, which are differentiated when appropriate.
- Identifying and organising appropriate trips, visitors and resources.
- Informing parents about the topic via the notice board and inviting them to become involved.

Our medium-term planning covers a period of weeks, usually a half term. Many activities are naturally cross-curricular and enable work to take place within a meaningful context. A planning grid shows intended learning experiences for each week (Table 7.3). These plans are flexible so that the children's interests can influence the direction the theme takes.

During a topic about autumn, the Reception class visited Stourhead Gardens. The children thoroughly enjoyed seeing all the different types of trees, playing in the leaves and collecting conkers and seeds. On our return to school the sand tray was filled with some of the leaves we had collected. Some of the children used the sticks and leaves to make shelters for the toy animals. They noticed that some animals were able to hide better than others. This led to looking at big books about camouflage. The children brought in soft toy animals from home and used recycled materials to make shelters or houses for them. This activity presented an opportunity for the teaching of specific skills such as folding and cutting card to make doors and windows. The children drew on their previous experience of colour mixing with powder paints to mix the right colours to 'hide' their animals. This adaptation was so successful that it is now part of the 'Colours' topic.

Adapting planning in this way ensures that the needs, interests and achievements of the children are considered. Changes to the length or content of the topic, successful or unsuccessful activities, and suggestions or comments that will be useful for informing future planning, are recorded in the topic review. In addition to the week-by-week planning grid, medium-term plans are made to cater for children with additional educational needs. The *Curriculum Guidance for the Foundation Stage* explicitly supports inclusion:

Table 7.3: Example of a medium-term plan for the Foundation Stage

Spring	Week 1	Week 2	Week 3	Week 4	Week 5	Week 6
PSED	Planning – 3 activities and discuss plan with adult C. time – fruit salad	What makes us feel happy/sad C. time – all change Birthday game Favourite things	What makes us feel angry, frightened C. time – pass a smile Faces 2	We are all special and good at different things C. time – oranges and lemons Teach me a game	People we care about – friends and family C. time – all change Pass a smile Special friends	Easter/spring/new life Special things to us and to others
CLL	Begin to make a book about ourselves Introduce M. Waddell Non-fiction books – labels	Make a book of things we like Write list of favourite food	Make up silly rhymes for our bodies – arm, etc. Write a letter home to ask for baby photo	Make a speech bubble, I'm brilliant/great at… Re-tell a favourite story	Write about ourselves for class book – ICT	Re-tell Owl Babies story Write message in Easter card
MD	Count and sort children in the class Sort face pictures	Bring in a favourite cuddly toy – sort, count, weigh and measure toys Fav. colour graph	What can you do in 1 minute? – jump, draw, etc. Fav. fruit graph	How far can you throw a bean bag/jump? Make handspan rulers	Mark heights on wall, find things taller/shorter than you	Make a hat the right size for your head Build tal /short models
KUW	Read books about the body Draw and label body parts Discuss seasons, winter and spring	Read books, discuss our senses – eyes Go for a walk, what can we see Make a chair/	Senses – taste and smell Taste fruits, which do you like Identify food from smell pots	Senses – listening walk, identify sounds What do we need to help us grow and keep healthy?	Senses – touch Feel different textures Make rubbings of diff. surfaces	Walk to look for signs of spring using all our senses Design a hat for Easter

Table 7.3: (cont.)

Spring	Week 1	Week 2	Week 3	Week 4	Week 5	Week 6
KUW (cont.)		house/car the right size for your toy		Display baby photos – how have we changed?		
ICT	My World	Toybox	Toybox	Roamer	Digital camera	My World
PD	'Time to move' – It's your move – Awareness of body parts	'Time to move' Part 2	Moving fast and slow, feel heartbeat after running, stopping and starting	Travelling on hands and feet Stop and touch different body parts	Make up a dance, how do we move when we feel happy, sad, etc.	Continue activity from week 5
CD	Drawing ourselves, and pictures for book Percussion sounds – Busy body song	Wax and wash name cards Duration – steady beat Clap rhythm of our name	Obs. drawing – toys Steady beat with nursery rhymes	Colour mixing handprints Design cards for Mothering Sunday	Mark-making with inks Finger-painting listening steady beat to music	Obs. drawing – flowers Make Easter cards Listening to and repeating sounds

Early years practitioners have a key role to play in working with parents to identify learning needs and respond quickly to any area of particular difficulty, and to
develop an effective strategy to meet these needs, making good use of individual
education plans, so that later difficulties can be avoided.

(QCA/DfEE 2000: 18)

These individual education plans (IEPs), to which parents contribute, provide more
detailed medium-term planning for children with additional educational needs.

Short-term planning

Weekly plans are displayed on the parents' notice board and show the resources and
activities that will be available each day. In the nursery, resources in the activity areas
are changed daily, in the Reception class they are changed weekly. The activities are
adapted according to the children's needs and interests, and are influenced by assessment and observation of children's responses. Within this framework children are
able to incorporate their own ideas and are free to add their current favourite
resource to the activity. For example, when playing in the sand, Natalie, James and
Geri in the Reception class had invented a game involving dinosaurs. Each week
when the sand activity changed (dry sand and wheels one week, wet sand and
moulds the next) the children collected the dinosaurs and built the changes into
their game. They were still learning about the nature of dry and wet sand while
being able to be creative and use their initiative.

Of course, each setting will develop its own way to present weekly planning.
Another school in the same local authority area uses the format in Table 7.4. Here
we can see that *The Very Hungry Caterpillar* by Eric Carle provides numerous opportunities for a 'science' topic to enrich all areas of learning. The teachers in this school
have identified learning goals or, where appropriate, the stepping stones that will be
reached along the way. This is supplemented by a plan showing how sand, water
and other ongoing activities will be offered to the children. The format also includes
National Numeracy and Literacy Strategy objectives. Early in the Reception year
most learning objectives will relate to the stepping stones rather than the goal – later
in the year the goals are within reach!

In addition there are plans for ongoing activities, which reflect the importance of
free play. These activity plans (Table 7.5) include Early Learning Goals and learning objectives that are linked with the appropriate area of learning, for example
knowledge and understanding of the world.

Day-to-day observations and assessments of the children are used to inform the
daily plans. These plans deal with the implementation of learning experiences, identifying specific learning objectives and differentiation. They also identify where the
adults are working, questions and vocabulary they might use, and the planned intervention for individuals or groups of children.

Table 7.4: Example of weekly planning in the Foundation Stage: *The Very Hungry Caterpillar*

Area of learning		What do we want the children to learn?		How will we enable this learning to take place?			How will we know who has learned what? What next?	
		Learning intentions based on stepping stones/ELGs	*Vocabulary*	*Activities (+ links with other aspects of learning)*	*Extension activities*	*Special resources*	*Assessment*	*Notes on how assessment will inform future planning*
PSED	SS2	Show care and concern for others, for living things and the environment		Look for minibeasts and treat them appropriately	Discuss our role within the environment	Magnifying glasses		
	ELG	Maintain attention, concentrate and sit quietly when appropriate		Class sessions – carpet times and group work				
CLL	ELG	Listen with enjoyment and respond to stories		Enjoy the story of *The Very Hungry Caterpillar* Enjoy re-telling the story to a group or with a talking partner	Illustrate/write a section of the story	*The Very Hungry Caterpillar* (V.H.C.) book		
	ELG	Explore the meanings of new words		Discuss the story and the life cycle of a butterfly (KUW)				
	SS2	Respond to what they have heard by relevant comments, questions and actions		Explore language when outside looking for minibeasts, LSA to note good use of language (KUW)	Make lists of what they find			
	ELG	Hear, say and attempt to write the dominant phonemes in words		Have a 'treasure hunt' to find cards with food items depicted. Must find the food item in the correct order to follow the story (MD)	Opportunity to make their own zig-zag books of a sequence of events			
	LI	Sequence the events of a story		Enjoy non-fiction books in the book corner	Use internet to search for articles about minibeasts			
	LI	Begin to understand the use of non-fiction texts		Appointment diary in role-play area				

Area	Code	Learning objective	Activity	Notes	Resources
MD			Phonic groups – Jolly phonics and tricky words		
	NSLO	To know the days of the week	Cards of days to put in order Retell the V.H.C. story (CLL)	Write and/or read days of the week	A set of cards with a variety of patterns drawn on – e.g. spots, spirals, etc. Cards should be in black and white
	SS1	To begin to recognise and recreate simple patterns (and sequences)	Sequencing of story (CLL) Play 'pattern snap'	Make their own pattern of events over time	
	ELG	In practical activities and discussion begin to use the vocabulary involved in adding and subtracting	Folens pre-school programme. Unit 10 activity 3a – Butterflies		
	NSLO	To understand the concept of more than/ less than related to capacity	Structured play activities involving a variety of containers in the water tray	Extend by questioning as appropriate	Water tray and containers
KUW		Discuss the life cycle of a butterfly	Folens Reception science		
PD		Move with control and co-ordination	A dance story based around the movements of minibeasts in the garden Ongoing games sessions outside if possible	See link with CD	
	ELG	Wriggling Swooping Crawling Sliding			
CD	SS3	Explore the different sounds of instruments	Dance of minibeasts (PD)	Children to use instruments to make appropriate minibeast noises	
	SS3	Work creatively on a small scale	Symmetrical butterfly paintings (MD)	Introduce the idea of symmetry	

Table 7.5: Example of an activity plan in the Foundation Stage

Task: Free play with water and floating and sinking materials.

Resources:

A range of floating and sinking objects, e.g. shells, pebbles, sponges, corks, cups, plasticine, boats, ice.

Organisation:

Children to wear blue water aprons.

Resources available for children to select.

Children able to:

Choose to participate.

Handle objects safely and with increasing control.

Work as part of a group or class, taking turns and sharing fairly.

Select and use activities and resources independently.

Early learning goals:

Investigate objects and materials by using all of their senses as appropriate.

Ask questions about why things happen and how things work.

Maintain attention and concentration.

Learning objectives:

Experience of materials ~ To understand that some objects float in water.

To understand that some objects sink in water.

To understand that some objects absorb water.

To sort objects according to whether they float or sink.

Investigative skills ~ To observe using senses.

To communicate ideas to friends or adult.

To compare similarities and differences.

To use equipment in appropriate way.

To experiment.

Teaching points *(if an adult is available)*:

Encourage independence (putting on own apron or asking a friend to help, selecting resources, making decisions about how to use them, hanging up apron when finished).

Introduce or extend vocabulary, e.g. float, sink, soak, under, on, top, bottom, up, down, half way, quickly, slowly.

Ask questions, e.g.

What is it made of?

What do you think will happen? Do you think it will float? Do you think it will sink?

Does it sink all the way to the bottom? Does it float right at the top?

What happens when you push it under the water?

What do you notice about the things that float?

Extension activities:

What happens if you change the shape of the object, e.g. plasticene, paper?

Can you make a boat? What material will you use?

Can you make something that floats, sink?

Making predictions (Which objects do you think will float?)

Planning for effective adult intervention

In order to ensure effective adult intervention that enhances learning, we believe it is essential that all adults working with children understand and share the ethos of the Early Years setting. We aim to achieve this shared understanding in a number of ways. Teaching staff, nursery nurses and classroom assistants meet as a team to discuss current issues and concerns such as observations of children's responses, activities that have worked well, and future plans. A common approach along with knowledge of individual children helps to ensure that any intervention is sensitive and appropriate. We also produce adapted versions of our activity plans (Table 7.5) to guide adults working with children.

As we have seen in Chapter 5, interventions should always be informed by observations of children's actions. The first cameo below shows that observation can lead to interventions 'there and then' while the second illustrates how small yet important additions to daily plans can be informed by them.

Susie enjoyed riding bikes, drew and painted using circular marks, used wheels with dry sand and was fascinated with turning taps on and off. She had worked briefly with the water with little interest. When nursery staff provided old bicycle wheels, she became very excited and was determined to make the water turn the wheel. She tried to balance the wheel on the edge of the water tray and then carefully put gutters across to support the wheel. The nursery nurse working with her observed without intervening. This was unstable and although the wheel frequently slipped and fell, she persevered for several attempts. The nursery nurse said, 'It keeps wobbling, doesn't it? I wonder if there is something that would make it more steady?' The child looked around and eventually found that the milk crates formed a stable base to support the wheel, exclaiming 'That's it! That's not wobbly now! I done it, look!' She called the nursery nurse to see the wheel turning. The nursery nurse responded, 'That's fantastic! What is making your wheel turn?' The child replied excitedly, 'The water. The water goed on the top and it goed round and the wheel goed round and round like that.'

As part of a topic on gardens, the role-play area in the nursery was turned into a garden centre, the children planted seeds, played with compost in the sand tray and enjoyed filling up flower pots with compost. Real plants and artificial flowers were on sale in the garden centre. Lily went to the art area, using collage materials available, scissors and glue; she collected a large piece of paper, cut a long strip, which she used to make the stem of a flower. She collected a small piece of paper, put some glue over it, folded it over the top of the stem and decorated it with collage materials to make a flower. She then made several more flowers, which she put in the garden centre to be bought by other children. The next day we put some long art straws in the art area, without saying anything, so Lily and her friends made some more flowers.

Involving parents and carers

Our ethos and philosophy is shared with parents and carers on our home visits, which take place prior to the children's entry to the Nursery and Reception class. It is also published in our Foundation Stage booklet of information for parents. We share our planning with parents: medium-term and weekly plans are displayed on the parents' notice board and they are invited to become involved.

During a topic about toys, a parent read the plans on the notice board and offered to bring in his collection of old toys. He talked to the whole class, showing them each toy and encouraging them to ask questions and share their own experiences. The children then played with the toys and became very interested in the moving toys, particularly the robots. In the following days the children explored moving toys, they designed and made robots with recycled materials and Duplo, and incorporated robot role-play into their games.

The activity plans mentioned above (Table 7.5) are very useful for explaining to parents and other visiting adults the purpose of the children's activities and for demonstrating how they link with the Foundation Stage curriculum. As you can see from the example, these plans also give specific guidance for appropriate adult intervention. All parents are encouraged to help at the school, and parents working in the Foundation Stage have shown a lot of interest in these activity plans and found them to be very informative, although this was not their original intention. We have therefore developed a 'guidance for helpers' sheet which gives them key information about how to work with the children effectively.

Summary

We have shown in this chapter how we begin our planning by developing a clear and shared set of aims for our Foundation Stage curriculum. We aim to establish an engaging learning environment, organising and drawing on resources inside and outside the classroom. We then plan a coherent and appropriate range of experiences for the children in our school, progressively refining and adapting our approach through long-, medium- and short-term plans. We are always mindful of responding flexibly to children's interests and enthusiasms, which are identified through careful observation of the ways in which children interact with others and the learning environment. Parents have a key role in supporting children's learning, but they too need support. Our responsibility is to communicate our aims, objectives and plans to all the adults in the class so they can join us in educating the children in the best possible way.

CHAPTER 8

What do I need to know?

Science and D&T subject knowledge for Early Years practitioners

Dan Davies

Purpose of this chapter

Through reading this chapter you will gain

- an appreciation of the role of subject knowledge in your science and D&T practice
- appropriate scientific understanding to support your interventions in young children's learning
- information to help develop your D&T expertise in order to support young children's learning in this area.

Introduction

Primary practitioners' subject knowledge has been a vexed topic of debate for some time (see e.g. Davies and Allebone 1998). The introduction of the National Curriculum exposed gaps in teachers' scientific understanding according to Alexander *et al.* (1992); findings which have led to the imposition of an increasingly knowledge-based training for primary teachers over the past decade. In contrast, we might argue that for Early Years educators, understanding of young children's development should take precedence over 'inappropriate' curriculum-related subject knowledge. Rosemary Feasey (1994) argues that this led to a *deficit model* of subject knowledge in Early Years science during the 1980s and '90s, with an emphasis upon activity for its own sake in which there was an imbalance between process and content. If we neglect young children's scientific understanding, or assume that it will simply develop naturally through engagement in scientific processes, we may be unwittingly reinforcing misconceptions which will hinder their later learning.

The two extremes in the process–content debate have become somewhat closer to reconciliation in recent years in the acknowledgement that teachers of young children need several different kinds of 'subject' knowledge. This includes what Shulman (1987) has called *pedagogical content knowledge* – understanding of the ways that children come to learn science and D&T combined with appropriate techniques to help them make sense of the information they are receiving. Pedagogical content knowledge forms the basis of the interventions we recommend in Chapters 9 and 10. It is important to recognise, however, that it is underpinned by teachers' own understanding of science and D&T: 'The interrelationship among teacher knowledge of science (and D&T), Early Years pedagogy and children's ideas is complex. Without a firm understanding of subject knowledge . . . the teacher is less likely to be able to incorporate the other two elements successfully' (Feasey 1994: 87). How *much* knowledge we possess may be less important than the *depth* of our grasp of the basics. For example, the ability to quote Archimedes' Principle is of less use to the Early Years practitioner than to be able to explain in different ways why some objects float and others sink. Similarly, technical knowledge about raising agents is less relevant than knowing how much yeast to add to a bread mixture. The scientific and D&T knowledge we need falls under three main headings: *conceptual* (our understanding *of* and *about* science and D&T), *procedural* (the skills we need to 'do' science and D&T successfully) and *attitudinal* (our emotional responses to these areas and attributes needed for success). Of course, all of these elements of learning need to interweave with one another; we need positive and questioning *attitudes* to make best use of our *skills* in exploring and investigating phenomena to gain *understanding*, which will in turn inform our *attitudes* and *skills*. In this chapter, we will look at each aspect in turn in relation to both science and D&T.

Attitude problem?

I will start by considering our attitudes, since these are often the key to developing secure skills and concepts. Our attitudes towards science and D&T often stem from our own educational experience; if this was narrow, didactic or gender-stereotyped we may approach the subjects with fear, antipathy or misapprehensions as to their true nature. Women particularly may have had their confidence undermined by negative experiences in their own science education (Johnston 1996). Not only is it likely that our attitudes will be transmitted to children in the way that we approach science and D&T, but lack of confidence will limit our ability to challenge and develop children's ideas. According to Harlen and Holroyd (1995), teachers with low confidence in science tend to rely heavily on worksheets and kits, with an emphasis on 'telling' rather than discussing the outcomes of exploration.

As practitioners, we need to move beyond the constraints of our own educational experiences, which may have left us with the impression that science is about 'getting the right answer', or that D&T is concerned with 'making things that look nice'. There are several specific attitudes related to both areas that we might wish children to develop; the best way of achieving this is to demonstrate those same attitudes ourselves. Harlen (2000) reminds us that attitudes are 'caught not taught', and goes on to suggest a number of ways in which we can model curiosity, respect for evidence, willingness to change ideas and critical reflection – all of which say something about the nature of the subject (see Chapter 1). I have added D&T-related examples to her suggestions:

- Demonstrate *curiosity* by showing an interest in new things, particularly those children have brought in from home. If you have recently bought a product that you're particularly pleased with or think has been well designed, bring it in and show it to the children. 'I'm really interested in how it does this . . .' 'I wonder how this part works . . .'

- Show *respect for evidence* by admitting to children when activities do not turn out as you expected. For example, say 'That's really interesting, I was expecting the water to go through that fabric,' rather than trying to 'gloss over' the experiment that seemed to 'go wrong' by telling them what should have happened! Similarly, do not be afraid of admitting when something you have made fails to fulfil its function. Use it as an opportunity for children to suggest ways you could improve it, rather than 'brushing it under the carpet'.

- Tell children about times when you have *changed your ideas* about a scientific principle, e.g. 'I used to think it would be easier to swim in the deep end because the water holds you up more, but when I saw that things float just the same in shallow or deep water I had to think again.' Again, if something unexpected happens when children are exploring an aspect of science (for example, electric circuits often throw up surprises!) admit that you will have to come up with a new explanation. This is not an admission of failure, it is an important demonstration of how science works! In D&T, if you are making something with children – perhaps in the construction area – make a point of having to take something apart and try it a different way because your original design did not seem to be working.

- *Critical reflection* is an attitude displayed in abundance by many educational practitioners; indeed we are often over-critical of our own performance. However, critical reflection is not about focusing on the negative; we can start by identifying our scientific and technological successes. For example, in my work with primary teachers they are frequently surprised by how well they are able to describe everyday phenomena in scientific terms, or their aptitude in constructing models with simple mechanisms. The key to critical reflection is to recognise our strengths in these areas and build on them, while recognising that any scientific procedure or D&T product can always be improved. Look at some of the things you use every day and consider simple adaptations or alternative choices of material that would improve the product. Also think about reasons why designers may not have included your innovation – price, fashion or options for product development perhaps?

In addition to reflecting on the specific attitudes outlined above, it is well worth trying to articulate your own beliefs about science and D&T, to act as guiding principles for your work in the classroom. Try to encapsulate each in a single sentence, e.g. 'I think science is all about . . .', then compare your views with those expressed in Chapter 1. Letting your beliefs about early childhood education infuse those about science and D&T – leading perhaps to the inclusion of words such as creativity and co-operation in your definitions – will go a long way towards developing attitudes that will be helpful to you in your work with children.

Skills shortage?

I turn next to the procedural knowledge we need in order to guide and support young children's active engagement in science and D&T. I find it helpful to categorise such knowledge under three headings, ranging from broad understanding of how to go about a science or D&T project to the individual skills needed:

- *Procedure level.* This is the 'big picture' of the stages we need to go through to explore or enquire scientifically, or to develop a design idea into a finished outcome. Those of you familiar with the structure of *The National Literacy Strategy* (DfEE 1998a) might find it helpful to consider the analogy with *text level* work – the emphasis is on the meaning of the whole.
- *Thinking skill level.* Thinking skills are those with a high cognitive content, promoted in Curriculum 2000 (DfEE/QCA 1999a: 22) as important in helping children 'learn how to learn'. They include the skills involved in information-processing, reasoning, enquiry, creative thinking and evaluation. I hope it will be clear that each of these areas is of direct relevance to both science and D&T. They are sometimes referred to as 'process skills' (e.g. Harlen 2000), which in combination with each other make up the procedures referred to above. Examples that might fall under the 'enquiry' heading include hypothesising, modelling and planning, each of which might play a different role in either a scientific or D&T process. To use the literacy analogy, they are the sentences that make up the text.
- *Motor skill level.* Motor skills include the ability to measure using a ruler, or to cut a piece of fabric using a pattern. They involve thought as well as action, but are generally less abstract than the thinking skills described above. They are the 'nuts and bolts' of science and D&T processes ('words' in the literacy analogy) without which we would be unable to use our thinking skills effectively. Scientists, designers and technologists need to be 'hands-on' people as well as big thinkers. In my experience of working with primary teachers, it is often in the use of equipment that they feel least confident, so it is here that I will start.

Skills for using equipment and working with materials

Interestingly, most science subject support books for primary teachers focus on conceptual knowledge, to the virtual exclusion of skills and techniques, whereas the opposite is generally true in D&T. Two useful sources of D&T skills support are the *DATA Helpsheets* (DATA 1999b) and *The Design and Technology Primary Co-ordinators' File* (DATA 1996). I have drawn upon both of these publications in the guidelines which follow (Table 8.1), which cover teachers' requirements to the end

Table 8.1: Developing your motor skills in science and D&T

Motor skill	Tools/equipment	Suggestions/notes
Making holes	Single hole punch	Can be used on paper, card, corrugated plastic (corruflute), lolly sticks. Holes can be rather large for split pins. Only for punching holes up to 3 cm from the edge of material.
	Paper drill	Use with a block of wood or cutting mat underneath the material. Can make three sizes of hole, but the smallest bit easily becomes blocked with paper circles.
	Hand drill	For thicker wood and card. Select size of bit carefully. Clamp work to table with a block of wood underneath. Best to use with a drill stand.
Cutting and shaping	Scissors	Cut roughly to shape before fine detail. Keep scissors for fabric separate. If cutting a slot, use a hole punch to start.
	Snips	Heavy duty scissors for thick card, corruflute and heavy fabric. Use a thick elastic band around handles to reduce distance for small hands to stretch.
	Junior hacksaw	Use with a wooden bench-hook over the edge of table (commercial versions have slots for square section wood and dowel). Cuts on the push, not on the pull. Do not blow sawdust, as it can get into eyes.
	Glass-paper (sandpaper)	Wrap round a block and use to smooth rough ends after sawing or drilling.
	Food knife	Round-ended, serrated knives are safest. Use with an anti-bacterial chopping board. Cut fruit and vegetables in half to provide flat surface.
	Juicer, peeler, grater	All need strength and fine motor co-ordination.
	Pastry cutters	Carefully washed plastic pots can be used.
Joining	Pritt Stick	Only useful for very light work (not mechanisms). Avoid over-application and over-extension.
	PVA glue	Bonds card/wood/corruflute/fabric but long drying time. Decant into film canisters (resealable) with spreaders. Avoid over-application and support while drying.

Table 8.1: (*cont.*)

Motor skill	Tools/equipment	Suggestions/notes
	Copydex	Smelly, but useful for joining fabrics.
	Glue gun	Use only low-temperature guns (educational suppliers). Instant but brittle bond.
	Card triangles ('Jinks' joints')	Strengthen joins between wood (especially if fixed using glue gun). Use PVA to apply.
	Sticky tape	Try to minimise use to improve finish. Useful for hidden parts (e.g. slider mechanisms in card) or joining temporarily while glue dries.
	Pipecleaners	Make flexible joints between two straws or pieces of corruflute (end to end).
	Wire	Use thin garden wire to join two pieces of thicker wire/pipecleaner/dowel.
	Dowel	Many wheels push fit onto dowel. Can also be used to join corruflute end to end.
	Split pins (paper fasteners)	Join flat materials with holes where swivel movement is required. Fold over ends to reduce sharp hazard.
	Needle and thread	Use plastic needles with large eyes in loose-weave fabric initially. Double thread and knot ends together to reduce re-threading!
	Stapler	Useful for paper, card and fabric under adult supervision.
	Clothes peg	Useful for holding work together while glue dries, or for joining moving axle to vehicles.
Drawing	Pencil/pen	If you think you 'can't draw' do not be discouraged – aesthetic appeal is not necessary! Match the type of drawing to its purpose: rough sketches for initial ideas; observation drawings to record features of interest (annotate if necessary); parts drawings to aid making, showing how bits fit together.
	ICT graphics programs	Non-specialist software such as Word and Paint can be useful for combining standard shapes and lines, with labels. Children's versions (e.g. Kid Pix) are similar. 3-D drawings using simple shapes can be produced using software such as Tabs+ (Aspex software).

Table 8.1: (*cont.*)

Motor skill	Tools/equipment	Suggestions/notes
Measuring/ observing	Hand lens/ bug box	Store carefully – can easily become scratched. Finding the distance for focus can be difficult – lenses on stands and bug boxes overcome this.
	Ruler/tape measure	Ruler and tape measure scales starting at the very end reduce errors. Young children sometimes start measuring from '1'.
	Sand timer	Only useful for pre-set times. Difficult to tell when it has finished. Children sometimes turn over before the end!
	Stopwatch/ stopclock	Electronic stopwatches are tricky – finding the right function, pressing the right buttons at the right time, interpreting the complex reading. Easier to use a clockwork stop-clock!
	Beaker, measuring jug, measuring cylinder	Avoid parallax error by reading with eye at liquid level. Rounding up or down to faded scales is tricky and needs support.
	Beam balance	What counts as balanced? Sometimes it depends where you put the objects in the pans!
	Scales	Reading scales demands high-level numeracy skills.
	Thermometer	Choose the right range for the temperatures likely to be measured. Avoid mercury. Wait for the thermometer to adjust to the temperature of liquid before taking readings. Scales again!

of Key Stage 1. If you need to see pictures of any of the equipment mentioned, please refer to either of the DATA resources.

Thinking skills for science and D&T

Although science subject knowledge books aimed at teachers tend to focus on conceptual understanding, there are examples of support to develop process skills, such as the *Letts QTS Science for Primary Teachers Audit and Self-study Guide* (Peacock 1998), written to resource the National Curriculum for Initial Teacher Education (DfEE 1998b). I have drawn upon it in compiling Table 8.2, which indicates the ways in which process skills can be used differently in science and D&T.

Table 8.2: Developing your thinking skills in science and D&T

Thinking skill	Examples in science	Examples in D&T
Questioning	'What happens if…' questions, inviting comparison of one set of conditions with another, e.g. 'Do beans sprout best in the light or dark? What is the best temperature for sprouting beans?' Also, survey-type questions and information-seeking, e.g. 'Why does the moon have phases?'	Questions about people's needs and preferences, e.g. 'Which flavour jelly do most people prefer? How could we improve our playground?' Questions about an object/ product, e.g. 'How does it work? How was it made? How long will it last?'
Hypothesising, predicting and guessing	I *hypothesise* that the red car will travel faster than the blue one because its wheels are smoother and I think smooth wheels cut down friction (based on theory or generalisation). I *predict* that the blue car will beat the red because it did last time (based on prior experience). I *guess* that the red car will go faster than the blue one (no basis).	A design idea can be like a hypothesis, e.g. 'I think this will be the best shape for a computer mouse, because it fits a wide range of hand measurements comfortably, and people generally prefer holding smooth, rounded objects to sharp, angular ones.' Alternatively, it can be a guess or hunch, but usually based on some previous experience or intuition.
Modelling	Modelling the flow of electricity round a circuit, perhaps by using an analogy or a kinaesthetic experience (e.g. 'being' a circuit), building understanding of an abstract concept which is itself a model of a physical phenomenon.	Modelling ideas for a new kind of torch, either mentally or through drawings and scrap materials is a process of trying to refine and develop initial ideas.
Planning	For a 'fair test' type of investigation, need to select: *Independent variable* (what I will change, e.g. temperature) *Dependent variable* (what I will observe or measure, e.g. height of bean plant)	Planning for making involves listing all the tools, materials and components that will be needed, sometimes in 'exploded' diagrams showing how all the parts fit together. It might be necessary to

Table 8.2: (*cont.*)

Thinking skill	Examples in science	Examples in D&T
	Control variables (what I will try to keep the same, e.g. type of bean, light conditions, amount of water).	produce a flow chart showing the steps to be taken in sequence. Planning for mass production involves turning this into a system.
Interpreting	Using previous scientific knowledge to make sense of data (in the form of observations, tables or charts), sometimes using 'er' statements, e.g. 'The warmer the temperature, the faster the bean plant grows (until it gets too hot!).'	Interpreting test data, e.g. 'My wind-powered buggy travelled slowly because the surface area of the sail was too small, and perhaps there was too much friction between the wheels and axle.'
Evaluating	Did the enquiry help to answer the original question? If not, were there ways we could have improved our data collection methods, or been more careful in selecting our variables?	Did our finished outcome meet our expectations and the needs or wants of the people it was designed for? Are there ways we could improve the process or product?

Putting it all together

Developing our *procedure level* understanding will include using several of the thinking skills described above in a particular sequence, depending on the particular project and our own 'cognitive styles', e.g. whether we prefer pictures or words, small steps or giant leaps. There are several published models of 'the experimental method' and 'the design process', each of which has its pros and cons both for our own understanding and ways in which we might seek to guide children. For example, in the model of scientific enquiry referred to by Peacock (1998) as the 'classic' view,

> scientists must first decide on the idea/theory/area they want to investigate. They try to collect all the evidence concerning that area of science. They then attempt a working hypothesis (see above) and test it by experiment. The hypothesis and the evidence are published. Other scientists test it by conducting experiments of their own. If just one of these refutes the original hypothesis then a new hypothesis is needed.

(p. 44)

This model has, of course, been challenged, notably by Kuhn (1970), who placed more emphasis on the social and cultural nature of the scientific 'community' in its acceptance of new 'paradigms'. Scientific theories in Kuhn's view are not *induced* from data but are socially constructed by people working individually and in groups, who tend to have an emotional attachment to their ideas long after contradictory evidence is found! This may ring some bells in relation to children's (and our own) reluctance to let go of preconceptions. Feyerabend (1994) has gone as far as rejecting the whole concept of a scientific method, arguing that science has historically progressed through a series of *ad hoc* hypotheses and *ad hoc* approximations by creative scientists working in an 'anarchistic' way to question accepted concepts. He dismisses the idea that science can be run according to fixed rules as a 'fairy tale' – perhaps supporting the emphasis upon unstructured exploration rather than rigid experimentation in Early Years settings.

Similarly, design methodology has been described in different ways, for example as a process of *analysis–synthesis–evaluation* (Jones 1980), or an 'interacting design loop' in which the designer keeps going back to previous stages in the process to refine and develop his or her ideas. Perhaps the most powerful model of D&T activity is that proposed by the Assessment of Performance Unit (APU) as the 'interaction of mind and hand' (Kimbell *et al.* 1991; and see Figure 2.1). Here the designer is engaged in a constant dialogue between his or her mental images and the actions of her hands. It is both active and reflective, 'hands-on' and 'minds-on', and articulates well with what we know about young children's designing (see Chapter 2).

Conceptual confusion?

We now turn to what many practitioners might consider the most problematic area in developing professional expertise in science and D&T. Our confidence in the concepts we explore with children is the key to identifying and challenging what Driver (1983) called their 'alternative frameworks' – the personal, intuitive ways of making sense of the world based on limited evidence and experience. Tables 8.3 to 8.9 offer some examples of children's common scientific ideas and appropriate adult interventions, mapped to the underpinning knowledge needed by the practitioner. I have included most science topics likely to be encountered in Early Years settings, and have drawn upon the very helpful *Nuffield Primary Science* 5–7 teachers' guides (Nuffield Foundation 1993). I hope you find these tables useful, though they will certainly not cover every eventuality, since young children's questions 'do not fit tidily into the constructs of science, even though they seem simple' (Fensham 1986: 34)!

If this all seems rather daunting, don't forget that the best way of gaining confidence in your own scientific understanding is through learning alongside children:

> Introducing materials for exploratory play . . . can be a less threatening entry route for both teachers and children. Activities based on the children's initial explorations and questions are both easier to build on and focus directly on the child's present levels of understanding.

> (Riley and Savage 1994: 143)

Table 8.3: Conceptual knowledge: Electricity

Children's common ideas	Suggested questions, interventions	Teachers' subject knowledge
Electricity: 'comes out of the plug' 'comes from the ground' 'comes from shops' 'comes from batteries'	Ask the children to bring in toys that use electricity. Which have to be plugged in? Which work using batteries? Can any work using both? Look around the classroom to find things that use electricity. What do you think the wires are for?	Electricity (current) involves the flow of billions of tiny particles (electrons) through conducting materials (e.g. metals). This movement can be *generated* by converting another form of energy (e.g. chemical energy in batteries, heat energy in power stations).
Lighting a bulb (lamp): 'It lights up by itself' 'It needs a wire' 'It needs a battery'	Explore a collection of bulbs, batteries and wires to try out children's ideas. When they have found a way to light the bulb, they could draw it. How many wires did you need? Where do they have to join on to? Have you made a circle/loop? Show the metal inside insulated wire.	There needs to be a complete circuit for the electricity (electrons) that are *already in* the battery, wires and bulb to start moving – like a bicycle chain. The bulb has two connections (base and side) so electrons can flow through the filament, heating it until it glows.

Activities in which there are no 'wrong' answers address a need for emotional security in science for both children and adults (Edgington 1998: 69). If this is you, be reassured; it is not necessary to know all the answers! For many children, being given some glib explanation in response to their question may

- not fit with their current level of understanding
- not be believed!
- shut down further enquiry.

Far better to have enough scientific understanding to guide children towards answering their own questions. Remember that 'to decide the action to take in the light of evidence about the ideas children have, it is necessary to keep in mind both the starting point and the general direction of the more widely applicable scientific ideas, which are the eventual goal' (Harlen 1996: 69).

But what of our conceptual knowledge in D&T? In one sense, designers and technologists can draw upon knowledge from any field which they feel is relevant, e.g. forces from science, aesthetics from art, past technologies from history, etc. Yet there are some areas of knowledge which are of particular importance to teaching

Table 8.4: Conceptual knowledge: Floating and sinking (static forces)

Children's common ideas	Suggested questions, interventions	Teachers' subject knowledge
'It sinks because it's heavy/ big'	Do all heavy things sink? Can you find any big things that float?	When objects are placed in water they experience an upward force called upthrust (try pushing a balloon into water to feel how strong it is).
'It floats because it's small/ light'	Do all small/light things float? Can you find any small/light things that don't float?	The more water an object displaces ('pushes away', i.e. the amount the water level goes up) the more upthrust it experiences. So objects with a large volume compared to their weight (i.e. low density) are more likely to float, because they displace more water. Plasticene made into a boat shape floats because the boat shape displaces more water than the original lump.
'It sinks because it's made of metal'	Do all metal things sink? (use e.g. a cake tin)	
'It floats because it's made of wood'	Do all wooden things float? (pitch pine and lignum vitae don't). Can you find things that float that are not made of wood?	
'It floats because it's spread out'	What happens if we spread this plasticene out? (sinks) What can you do to make this plasticene float? (make it into a boat shape with sides) Look at pond skaters.	The weight of water displaced (= upthrust) balances the weight of the plasticene boat. Some light objects that are denser than water (e.g. a needle) can be made to float because they rest on the 'skin' of the water (surface tension).
'It floats because it's got air inside'	'Will a sponge float if you squeeze it in the water?' 'Do boats have air inside?' Try using a long perspex tube filled with water to watch objects sink at different rates.	

Table 8.5: Conceptual knowledge: Moving things (dynamic forces)

Children's common ideas	Suggested questions, interventions	Teachers' subject knowledge
(in response to a moving toy) 'It just goes', 'It just stops'	Can you make it go faster/ slower? Can you make it stop?	All movement is begun and ended by a force (a push or pull). Forces can have four effects:
'Its wheels make it go'	Can things move without wheels? How do wheels help?	1. Start or stop a moving object. 2. Change its speed.
'It stops because it's tired'	'Can you make it go for a longer/shorter time?'	3. Change its direction. 4. Change its shape.

D&T, including our understanding of the characteristics of materials and the ways in which different mechanisms can control movement. Both of these areas have considerable overlaps with science and are closely linked with the discrete skills for using tools and equipment (see above). Young children's understanding of materials and mechanisms, together with any potential alternative frameworks, are much less researched than the science topics above. However, the *DATA Primary School-Based INSET Manuals* (DATA 1998a; 1999a) are an invaluable source of background knowledge in these areas and I have drawn upon them in Tables 8.10 and 8.11.

The lists of materials and mechanisms on pp. 118–19 are restricted to those usually encountered up to the end of Key Stage 1.

Summary

In this chapter I have covered the wide range of scientific and D&T knowledge required by the Early Years practitioner. Some of this goes well beyond that which will be directly taught to children, but is in my view necessary in order to give you the confidence to diagnose children's strengths and areas for further development, providing the necessary experiences to lead them forward, which will be the purpose of the next two chapters. I have grouped this knowledge under three main headings – *attitudinal, procedural* and *conceptual* which I hope has provided a structure within which you are able to audit and develop your own expertise as required. Also important is an understanding of the relationship between these different components. For example, in science we need to make links both within the conceptual field (e.g. between 'shadow formation' in light and 'opacity' in materials) and between the conceptual and procedural (e.g. the link between the process skill of 'predicting' and the ideas about phenomena on which predictions are based). Links between our science understanding and D&T are also crucial to an interactionist approach, which is why I have treated them side-by-side in this chapter.

Table 8.6: Conceptual knowledge: Living things

Children's common ideas	Suggested questions, interventions	Teachers' subject knowledge
Living/ was alive/ never lived *It's alive because:* 'It moves' 'It's got eyes and legs' 'We use it' 'It feels soft'	Can you think of things that move/we use/are soft but are not alive? (make a collection) Can it grow? (N.B. some non-living things can grow) What about this worm?	Characteristics of living things: 1. *Nutrition* (feeding, or making food through photosynthesis) 2. *Respiration* (releasing stored energy in food – even green plants do this)
Animals: 'have got four legs and fur' 'These go together because they all live in water/sky/ under the ground.'	Show pictures of reptiles, birds, fish, insects, etc. How are they like a cat? Can you think of other animals that live in water/sky that don't look like these?	3. *Growth* (getting bigger, more complex) 4. *Sensitivity* (response to stimuli, e.g. light) 5. *Movement* (fast or slow, in one place or many)
Plants: 'aren't alive' 'have flowers' 'Trees aren't plants' 'We need to look after them or they die'	Can you think of things a plant does that we do too? Can trees have flowers? What about this spider plant? Do we need to look after 'weeds'?	6. *Excretion* (removing waste products) 7. *Reproduction* (passing information to the next generation) Scientists classify living things into 'Kingdoms' including animals and plants, but also fungi, bacteria, etc.
Growth: 'You get bigger' 'Food makes you grow' 'It grows inside an egg' 'It's waiting to come out' 'It grows from a seed' 'It needs sunshine, water and soil'	Order pictures of adults/ children at different ages. Do we ever stop growing? Can you tell which part of your body has grown? Do we grow every time we eat? What do you think it looks like inside the egg/seed? Grow cress/beans without soil – what's happened?	Some plants (e.g. oak) keep on growing throughout their lives. Most animals stop at maturity. Eggs and seeds have food stores within them. However, once a green plant has put out its first pair of leaves it starts to make its own food through photosynthesis.

Table 8.7: Conceptual knowledge: Materials

Children's common ideas	Suggested questions, interventions	Teachers' subject knowledge
Material = fabric *Sorting materials:* 'These things go together because you cut things with them' (confusion between material and the object)	Look at materials like fabric, e.g. carpet, pvc. Can these be materials? Introduce the word 'fabric' – material made of woven threads. Use samples of material for sorting rather than recognisable objects.	Material is a general term for all matter. According to particle theory, all materials are made up of bits too tiny to see (atoms and molecules) held together by forces (bonds) of different strengths. Any property of a material (e.g. softness) depends on the arrangement of its particles and the strengths of the bonds between them. A red toothbrush uses the properties of its materials (flexibility, toughness) to clean teeth, but its function and colour are not properties.
'The stone feels soft' 'The cotton wool feels smooth' 'These go together because they're red'	Stroke for smoothness, press for softness. Does this wire wool feel smooth?' Can you squash it? Can you find (e.g. plastics) of different colours? Show ice, water, steam – how are they different?	
Changing materials: 'It's always been like that' 'You can't change it' 'Before it was dirty, now it's clean' 'Before it was new, now it's old'	Explore playdough or plasticene. Make cakes or bread. Melt chocolate. How have we changed it? When you have a bath, are you still the same underneath? What's happened to make it look old? What do you think it looked like before?	We can change the arrangement of particles within materials, using force (e.g. squashing, cutting, stretching) or heat (e.g. melting, boiling, burning). Sometimes this changes the form of the material (physical change, e.g. water, ice, vapour), sometimes it makes a new material (chemical change, e.g. flour to bread). Physical changes are *usually* reversible, chemical changes *usually* permanent.

Table 8.8: Conceptual knowledge: Light

Children's common ideas	Suggested questions, interventions	Teachers' subject knowledge
Sources of light: 'The sun' 'The light bulb' 'Torches and lamps' 'Shiny things' 'The moon' 'Fire, flames' 'Water'	What happens when it's cloudy?' When do we need to have the light on in the classroom? Make a 'dark cave' in the classroom and try out different sources. Put shiny objects in a dark box with a peephole. Can children see them?	Only true sources emit light (the filament of a bulb or gas in a fire/the sun/TV screen are luminous). Other objects reflect or scatter light (e.g. the moon, silver paper), but they don't emit their own light.
Shadows: 'It's my reflection' 'The sun makes them' 'I can jump on it'	How does your shadow look different from you? Try drawing your shadow Do other things have shadows? Use translucent objects (e.g. thin slices of fruit) to make shadows. Make shadow puppets. Tell the story of Peter Pan.	Shadows occur because the path of light (which travels in straight lines) is blocked by an opaque object. Translucent objects (and more than one coloured light) can produce coloured or grey shadows.
Reflections: 'A picture of me' 'In mirrors'	Draw how you think you can see yourself in the mirror. Shine a torch at a mirror – what is happening to the light from the torch?	Reflections occur when light bounces off a very smooth surface in a predictable way. Non-reflective surfaces scatter light in all directions.
Darkness/seeing objects: 'You can see it because it's colourful/shiny/bright' 'It will be dark because it's black' 'I can see it because I'm looking' 'Light comes out of our eyes'	Do you think you could see it in the dark? (use the dark box again) Has it disappeared? Can you still feel it?	We can only see something when light from it (if it is a source or reflecting/scattering light) enters our eye. If there is no light, we cannot see, since there is nothing to trigger the nerve cells in our retinas.

Table 8.9: Conceptual knowledge: Sound

Children's common ideas	Suggested questions, interventions	Teachers' subject knowledge
Making sounds: 'It makes a sound if you hit/ shake it' 'Animals make sounds' 'It makes a sound because it's made of wood' 'It makes a high sound' (meaning loud) 'It makes a low sound' (meaning quiet)	Use a collection of musical instruments that children can beat, pluck, blow and shake. How many different ways can you make a sound? Can you see anything moving when you make the sound? (use rice on a drum, tuning fork in water or with a table tennis ball) What sounds can you hear now? What do you think is making them? Can you make a high, quiet/ low, loud sound?	Sounds are made when objects vibrate, causing the air particles around them to start moving rapidly backwards and forwards. This movement ripples outwards in a *longitudinal wave*, which can travel through solids, liquids or gases. The rate at which the object vibrates (its frequency or pitch) gives us high or low sounds. The size of the vibration (amplitude or volume) gives us loud and soft sounds.
Hearing: 'You can only hear things when you're listening' 'It all goes in my ears'	Call the child's name when they are engaged in another activity. Did you hear me even though you weren't listening? Make ear trumpets to amplify sounds.	Sound waves travel in all directions, enter our ears and make our ear drums vibrate, sending electrical signals to our brains, which then select what to 'listen' to.

Table 8.10: D&T conceptual knowledge: Working characteristics of materials

Material	Characteristics/suggestions
Paper/card: A4 Sheets, different thicknesses Packages, reclaimed Corrugated card, Papier mâché, Art straws	A sheet material, easily cut and shaped. Low density. Rigidity increases with thickness. Absorbent and weakens when wet. Strength increases when folded, and can be made into 3-D shapes of great complexity and rigidity. Can be used for modelling and making simple mechanisms (e.g. pop-ups). Corrugated card is rigid along the corrugations, flexible across them. Complex 3-D shapes can be modelled from papier mâché, which makes a hard shell when dry. Art straws lose rigidity when bent or flattened, which can be frustrating for young children.
Plastic: Sheet polythene/acetate Plastic packages/tubs Corrugated sheets (corruflute)	A resistant sheet material, fairly easily cut and shaped. Low density. Rigidity increases with thickness and type. Non-absorbent and waterproof. Can be opaque, translucent or transparent, so useful for windows/shadow puppets. Melts if heated (not recommended!). Corruflute is colourful, low density and rigid – useful for cladding frameworks.
Wood: Square-section dowel (jellutong – 9 or 10 mm) Round-section dowel Lolly sticks Balsa Off-cuts	A resistant material, needing hacksaw and drill to cut and shape (apart from sheet balsa, which can be cut with scissors). Medium density, high rigidity (apart from sheet balsa) – more rigid along the grain than across. Absorbent after long immersion, but otherwise water-resistant. Jellutong is very useful for constructing frameworks, using Jinks' joints (see discrete skills in Table 8.1). Dowel and lolly sticks are good for mechanisms, including axles and levers.
Textiles: Felt Hessian, binca, scraps Cotton fabric Cotton wool Thread/wool Carpet	Sheet materials made from fibres with high flexibility (apart from carpet). Can be cut using sharp fabric scissors and joined using needle and thread, staples, glue, velcro, zips, studs. Range of textures, from rough to soft, furry. Felt will not fray, so can be used without hems. Water resistance and absorbency depends on construction and fibres. Good heat insulation – useful for clothing, furnishings (beds) accessories (bags, wallets).
Food: Bread, flour, yeast, fat Water, milk, juices Fruit, vegetables	Non-resistant, edible! Density, rigidity, texture, colour, etc. depends on type, but properties can be combined and changed with heat (e.g. flour, eggs, sugar to make cake). Use a dedicated set of utensils, wipe-down

Table 8.10: (*cont.*)

Material	Characteristics/suggestions
Sugar, eggs, chocolate	aprons and table covering, anti-bacterial spray, chopping boards and bowls.
Mouldable materials: Clay, 'new clay' Playdough, plasticene Wet sand	Non-resistant, malleable. Clay and 'new clay' can become rigid (though brittle) if allowed to dry or fired in a kiln. Useful for modelling ideas in 3-D, particularly smooth, organic forms. Use a range of sculpting tools, rolling pins, rakes, moulds, etc. to shape.

Table 8.11: D&T conceptual knowledge: Mechanisms

Mechanism	Function/suggestions
Hinge	A flexible joint which allows movement from side to side, backwards and forwards, up and down. Strips of scored card, tape, treasury tags or fabric hinges can be used.
Slide	An opening and closing joint which allows movement from side to side or up and down. Sliders need slots or guides (strips of card stuck at each end allowing and controlling movement beneath them).
Axle and wheel (gear) (pulley)	An axle is a rod on which one or more wheels will turn. A wheel is circular and rotates about a centre allowing linear movement from circular movement. Axles can be joined to vehicles yet allowed to rotate using clothes pegs, straws, triangles with holes. Using a short length of plastic tubing to fit tightly over the end of an axle prevents wheels falling off. Wheels can be made to fit tightly by increasing the axle diameter using tape. Gears (toothed wheels with mesh to change the speed of rotary movement) and pulleys (grooved wheels over which a string or belt can run) may be encountered in construction kits (e.g. First Gear).
Lever	A mechanism which allows a small force over a large distance to exert a greater force over a small distance, or vice versa. They are any shape but are always rigid and always pivot around a point. Use lolly sticks or strips of thick card, joined with split pins or plastic rivets.

CHAPTER 9

Developing children's scientific knowledge, skills and attitudes

Dan Davies

Purpose of this chapter

Through reading this chapter, you will gain

- understanding of different types of science and D&T activities within which we can intervene to promote scientific learning
- strategies for developing and challenging children's scientific concepts, skills and attitudes.

Introduction

Throughout the book we have recommended an interactionist approach to science and D&T teaching, yet it is important that as practitioners we recognise and develop the aspects of learning that are distinctively scientific and vice versa. In Chapter 10 we will look at design and technological learning, but in this chapter our focus is on moving children forward as young scientists. As in the last chapter, we will consider the attitudinal, procedural and conceptual elements of their scientific learning, which are of course deeply intertwined. For example, a child might show the attitude of perseverance in making a plasticene boat to test in water, exercising her process skills in predicting whether it will float or not. If it floats, her concepts about shape, materials and buoyancy may begin to change, which might affect the attitude with which she approaches the next floating and sinking activity, and so on. Our job as a skilled practitioner is to select the 'best' time and words to use in encouragement and challenge, to help her make these steps. In this chapter we will look at the kinds of activities we might select and the ways we might intervene to maximise scientific learning.

Types of activities and experiences

Throughout this book we have promoted experiential learning, often within a 'play' context. Yet there will inevitably be some types of direct experience that will be of more direct benefit than others in developing specific concepts, skills and attitudes. The notion that, simply by providing a set of resources within a stimulating environment, children will spontaneously 'discover' scientific principles has been discredited (Harlen 2000). As emphasised in Chapter 7, even non-directed activities need to be part of a carefully planned sequence, and the value of any experience we set up should be judged on the basis of its potential future pathways: 'We intervene to encourage and promote those experiences which are likely to be productive of further experiences and, conversely, to discourage and dissuade pupils from other less productive courses' (Blenkin and Kelly 1988: 13). For example, a water tray activity in which carefully chosen objects float at different levels may be more productive than one in which all have equal buoyancy, depending on the prior experience and observation skills of the children.

Most scientific activities in Early Years settings fall under the general heading of 'exploration' (Foulds *et al.* 1992; Johnston 1996). The beauty of exploration, or 'scientific play', is its responsiveness to children's immediate concerns and interests, promoting excitement, awe and wonder and thus encouraging the curiosity they need to become active scientists. Exploration implies a less systematic approach than investigation, enquiry and experimentation – terms in general use to describe hands-on scientific activities at Key Stage 1 and beyond. Children do not necessarily plan 'fair tests', take measurements and form hypotheses during exploration, though there should be a smooth transition to more formal scientific enquiry: 'exploration plays a vital part in the development of both Early Years scientific skills and knowledge and is a prerequisite for more in-depth development of skills and knowledge, especially in children of primary school age' (Johnston 1996: 26). Exploration can take different forms; all of it is carefully planned and provided for by the practitioner, but the degree of focus and structure can vary as implied by the following terms:

- 'guided' exploration (either child- or adult-initiated, in which the adult intervenes to question and suggest ways forward)
- 'structured' exploration (adult-initiated, with deliberate scaffolding of scientific skills, concepts or attitudes).

Fisher (1996) distinguishes between *child-initiated, teacher-initiated* and *teacher-intensive* activities (in which the teacher is directly and constantly engaged with children). The first of these, common in Early Years settings, offers practitioners many opportunities for science-related talk.

Intervening in play

Even within apparently 'free' exploration, there is a role for the practitioner to 'feed spontaneous structures with content, not necessarily found at home, or in the street or playground' (Athey 1990: 41). David (1999) reminds us that careful questioning, explaining and telling are not inconsistent with play as the main 'vehicle', though Bruce (1994) warns against using all play as an excuse for adult input. Playing with children can have several purposes (Edgington 1998):

- to encourage imitation (e.g. to demonstrate more appropriate use of equipment)
- to broaden knowledge (e.g. sitting in the 'dentist's chair' and asking: 'Can you look at my filling?')
- to challenge and extend thinking (e.g. by introducing incongruity such as the teacher in role as a crying police officer who is afraid of the dark).

Of course, we must tread carefully, as it is easy to stop the play altogether! One way to 'tune in' to children's play so as not to intervene inappropriately is to observe their 'schemas' (repeated patterns of action indicating underlying cognitive development – see Chapter 2). Once we have diagnosed their incipient intention (Bruce 1997), adults can support schemas with appropriate language and resources, as in the following example of a 'trajectory schema':

> Perry's teacher introduced paper aeroplanes and noted that Perry was fascinated by the vapour trails left in the sky by the aeroplanes which passed over the school. She brought in some streamers and he ran, with streamers unravelling behind him. She was helping him to make tangible a trajectory path rather like the aeroplane's vapour trail.
>
> (Bruce 1997: 86)

In making the invisible visible, Perry's teacher was engaged in a classic technique within science education for helping children reach a deeper level of understanding in a particular concept area. Other examples might include breathing on a mirror to show condensation of water vapour, or placing rice on a drum to show vibrations.

Guided exploration

Whatever the level of structure, we need to be clear about our expectations from children's scientific explorations. In the past, criticism has been levelled at Early Years science activities as being too narrow in range and focus (Foulds *et al.* 1992). In order to develop children's exploration, we first need to watch them carefully and probe their understanding sensitively with well-phrased questions (see below).

The process of finding out children's ideas is sometimes known as 'elicitation' (see Chapters 2, 5) and occurs during or after an 'orientation' phase in which children familiarise themselves with the materials or phenomena to be explored (Ollerenshaw and Ritchie 1997). An example of elicitation through exploration is provided by the following case study from a day nursery. The nursery worker, Angela, was keen to extend children's water play by introducing colours in an adult-initiated, guided exploration. Through the new experience she had provided, she sought to explore each child's understanding about light sources, using a range of question-types:

- *attention-focusing* – drawing children's attention to a feature of the experience or phenomena they might have overlooked
- *challenging* – inviting children to take a second look and rethink their initial statement

- *prompting* – inviting children to take an action of some sort, exploring the phenomena further
- *person-centred* – including the phrase 'do you think', often inviting prediction.

Case study: Colour and light in water

Nursery worker Angela Millar at Oak Tree Day Nursery, Bath, works with 'John' (age 3.6) 'William' (3.5) and 'Simon' (2.10) on a guided exploration activity in the water tray. The children take it in turns to fill the water tray from a jug:

Angela: If you watch, it's splashing as it hits the bottom of the tray. (attention-focusing question)

As the tray begins to fill, the stream of water from the jug begins to make small bubbles.

John: Look.
Angela: What can you see? (responding to child's initiative)
John: Bubbles, little bubbles.

Angela invites each child in turn to choose a food colour and add a few drops to a jug of water. First, Simon adds some blue colour to the jug. It forms a dense cloud of colour, beginning to diffuse throughout the water.

Angela: What's happening?
Simon: It's gone blue.
Angela: Is it all blue? (challenge, inviting a second look) What do we have to do to make it all blue? (prompt to action)
John: Mix it up.

Simon mixes the jug, then carries it to the water tray.

Angela: What do you think will happen to the blue water when we tip it in? (person-centred question, inviting prediction)
Children: Don't know.

They pour it in, then add a jug of green water.

Angela: What colours can you see?
John: Green and blue.
Simon: There's a rainbow in it.
Angela: Is there? What colours can you see? (picking up on child's interest)
Simon: Blue and orange and red and yellow.
John: It's lots of colours.
Angela: What colours did we put in . . . what colour have we ended up with? (trying to get children to make the link between the component colours and the mixture)
John: Yellow

Figure 9.1: Shining a torch through food colouring in the water tray

Angela gives the children a torch each, and encourages them to shine it on to the surface of the water.

    Angela: *Have a go at shining it up from the bottom.*

The children look at the light coming up through the water (Figure 9.1). Angela adds some more colour and it begins to swirl in the tray.

    William: *Ooo look at this one, it's got a swirly line all around here.*
    Angela: *See if you can follow the pattern with the torch. (encouragement to kinaesthetic learning)*

John returns with a 'sparkler' he has made from silver paper (it is mid-November).

    John: *See if you can light this sparkler . . . (shines the torch on it – Figure 9.2) You can!*

John starts to wave the sparkler over the water tray.

    Angela: *Can you see the sparkler in the water?*
    John: *I can see the light in it (there was a dim reflection of the sparkler, but the torch was much brighter).*
    Angela: *Can you see your sparkler underneath the water?*

Figure 9.2: 'Can you light this sparkler?'

John puts the sparkler under the water tray. Children agree that it is hard to see.

   Angela: Shine the torch on John's sparkler. Can you see it now? (challenging children's idea that the 'shiny' paper sparkler might be a source of light; they can only see it when a true source of light shines on it)

Simon and John start to shine their torches onto the wall, bowl and other objects.

> John: I can shine it on my head, on your head.
>
> Angela: Can you shine it through the apron? (challenge, bringing out concept of translucency)
>
> Angela: We're going to have a go outside in a minute. Then when it's dark later we're going to have another go. See if it's different.

Commentary

Although Angela initiated this activity, she was quick to pick up on the children's focus of attention and allow the exploration to move in an unanticipated direction. When John introduced the 'sparkler' she was aware that he was making the connection between torches and fireworks, so used this opportunity to probe his understanding about sources of light. By inviting him to wave the sparkler underneath the water tray and then to illuminate it with a torch she was challenging his idea that the 'shiny' paper might itself be a source of light. Such interventions require careful observation of children to determine the direction of their focus; an awareness of children's 'alternative frameworks' (Driver 1983) in the concept area concerned; and a certain degree of subject knowledge and understanding on the part of the practitioner (see Chapter 8).

Using design and technology activities to develop children's scientific ideas

As suggested in Chapter 1, design & technology can provide the meaningful contexts that young children need to begin to understand abstract scientific concepts. Whether D&T is the starting point for scientific enquiry, an activity to challenge and 'restructure' children's ideas, or the means of reinforcing prior learning through application, is not important. As the following example shows, engaging in designing and making can reveal children's alternative frameworks and provide adults with opportunities to 'scaffold' their learning towards a more scientific understanding. The topic area for the following case study (light) is the same as the previous example, but since these children are in a Reception class they are dealing with different concepts – those of darkness and seeing. This project had an additional contextualising feature that is characteristic of Early Years science and D&T in that it was introduced using a story book (for further examples see Chapter 4).

Case study: Dark caves

Reception teachers Di Rhodes and Margaret Harrison at Newbridge St John's CE Infants School, Bath, based their science and D&T topic around the book Can't You Sleep Little Bear? *by Martin Wadell. Di and the Reception team wanted to introduce children to the concept of darkness as the absence of light, and to allay some of their fears about the dark. They hoped that through building a class cave in the role-play area, children would realise that they need light to see (in the form of a torch or hole in the cave). These scientific concepts were reinforced through a Design and Make Assignment – designing a dark cave where Little Bear can sleep.*

Margaret (Adult) introduced the activity to a group of five children, including 'Sian' and 'Billy':

Adult: This is Little Bear from the story. How could we make him a bear cave?

Sian: I already know . . . put lots of scary things.

Billy: You might get lost, couldn't find your way out.

Adult: (Picking up from child's comment) Why couldn't you find your way out? (trying to elicit responses about darkness)

Billy: You might fall through the floor . . . or there's not a door.

Sian: Something in the way.

Adult: What is a cave?

Billy: A big rock, an oval shape . . . with a hole in it.

Adult: I've got lots of things (pointing to range of materials on table). What might we need?

Sian: Might need big scary bits of those (pointing to black netting fabric).

Adult: Why do you think it's a good colour?

Billy: It's dark (of course, the cave could be any colour inside if there was no light).

Adult: Why do you think caves are dark? (trying to elicit responses about lack of light)

Billy: Spooky. (a consequence rather than a reason!)

Adult: What did we do to make our class cave darker? (relating to children's own shared experience) Why did we put black paper on the windows?

Sian: It stops light coming through. (grasps concept)

Adult: (showing box) Can we make this box into a cave? What do we have to do to make it into a cave?

Billy: Stick lots of dark bits on. (Figure 9.3)

Adult: Where? On the outside? (does child distinguish between outside covering and inside conditions?)

Billy: All over.

Adult: What makes a cave dark?

Sian: Under the ground it's dark – no light. (further evidence that she has grasped the concept)

In Di's class, a group of children (including 'Mark' and 'Josh') is working on their caves.

Mark: (showing some sparkly fabric on the outside cave) There's rock crystals underneath.

Di: Could you see those if they were in the cave? (Does he understand that sparkly fabric reflects light, rather than being a source of light?)

Mark: Yes, 'cos the light from the door reflects. (good understanding) The bear cave can have fresh air and a bit of light to see where he's going. (understands that we need light to see)

Figure 9.3: 'Billy' selects dark coloured fabric for his cave

Di: How does the light get in?

Mark: By going through the door. Caves don't have doors that open and shut.

Di: (to Josh, noticing a tapering cylinder he's sticking to his cave) Tell me about this bit.

Josh: Telescope. (Figure 9.4)

Di: Put it on your model and look through. What does it look like?

Josh: Really dark.

Di: What do you need to make it see-through? (introducing concept of opacity, needing light to see)

Josh: A hole. I'm going to put something inside.

Di: Would it still be dark if it's got holes?
        Josh: No.

Di: Why would that stop it from being dark?

Josh: Light can't go through that, block the light. (beginning to grasp concept, but still some confusion)

Di: (to Josh) Will the bear be able to see in your cave?

Josh: He won't in mine because I've stuck this over the chimney. I think that's going to be a fire. (pointing inside)

Di: When the fire's alight in the cave do you think it will be light or dark? (probing understanding – does this child understand that sources of light can help us see?)

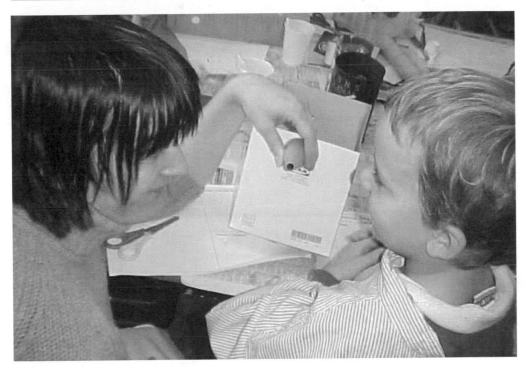

Figure 9.4: Di asks 'Josh' about the telescope on his cave

Josh: Light, um dark. (clearly confused by this question)

Di: On bonfire night, did you see a bonfire? (relating it back to recent experience) Was it really dark around the bonfire?

Josh: I saw it dark outside, it didn't go light (referring to the colour of the sky, rather than the effect of light from the fire – this misconception is raised in the story)

Di: (goes to fetch a torch) Let's pretend this torch is a fire . . . does it make it light?

Josh: But that fire's not real. The fire's not going to be on in there so it'll be dark (avoiding thinking through the consequences by rejecting the model!)

Commentary

The opportunity to engage children in talking about the caves they were designing and making enabled these teachers to probe understanding and relate the concept of darkness to other experiences, such as bonfire night. Selecting materials for the caves prompted discussion about whether colours could be seen in the dark, and the finished models enabled children to test their ideas about what they would be able to see. Throughout their interactions, Margaret and Di needed to

- Listen to the child – take what they say seriously;
- Try to understand what they mean;
- Use the child's meaning as the basis for the next adult comment, remark, suggestion or question;

- Try to speak or act in a way that the child understands.

(Siraj-Blatchford and MacLeod-Brudenell 1999: 113)

Discussing the words children are using (e.g. 'darkness', 'sparkly' from the activity above) can be a way of *restructuring* their ideas; another phase of a constructivist teaching framework meaning to challenge preconceptions or take understanding forward. For example, Di realised that Josh was equating darkness (absence of light) with black materials (those that reflect little light). Harlen (1996: 69) reminds us that children 'often use words with a restricted or idiosyncratic meaning, and by probing the meaning they have for words it may be possible to identify action to take'. Edgington (1998) noticed that children were using the word 'spider' to refer to a wide range of insects and other 'minibeasts', and was able to use secondary sources such as non-fiction picture books to challenge this definition. In considering when it is appropriate to introduce 'scientific words' to children, it is important that we establish the concept before attaching a name to it. For example, children need to experience and talk about pushes and pulls in a variety of contexts before the teacher can say, 'we call these forces'.

There are many ways to help children restructure their ideas in addition to discussion; Harlen (2000) recommends encouraging them to generalise from one context to another, extending the range of evidence available and providing opportunities for children to test their own ideas. Testing involves a more systematic approach – involving a specific set of skills – than is implied by the term 'exploration'. In the case study above, there was evidence of children using some of these scientific process skills such as observation and prediction, though the main procedural emphasis was on the skills involved in designing and making. It is to the development of the process elements of young children's scientific learning that we now turn.

From exploration to enquiry: developing children's scientific skills

Scientific exploration and enquiry form a continuum in young children's procedural progression. As children move into Key Stage 1, their motor skills will become finer so they can begin to be introduced to appropriate equipment for observation and measurement (hand lenses, balances, timers – see previous chapter). Their thinking skills will also become more sharply defined and sequenced; the beginnings of what the National Curriculum describes as scientific enquiry. Harlen (2000) identifies six key thinking skills in science (which she refers to as process skills): observing, hypothesising, predicting, investigating, interpreting and communicating, which the National Curriculum programme of study for science (DfEE/QCA 1999b) groups under three headings:

- Planning (asking questions, predicting, thinking about fair tests)
- Obtaining and presenting evidence (observing and measuring safely, communicating)

- Considering evidence and evaluating (making comparisons, identifying patterns, interpreting, reviewing)

It is worth emphasising that these thinking skills do not need to be undertaken in this order, neither do all of them need to feature in a particular enquiry. Particularly for young children, activities focused upon one or two skills, such as observing a spider carefully, are likely to be more developmentally appropriate than 'fair-test' type investigations which may be very time-consuming and teacher-intensive.

Indeed, observation has always been a central component of Early Years science, enabling children to focus on colour, texture, outline, shape, form, pattern, length, capacity and mass of interesting objects or living things. As children get older, measurement can play an increasing role in observation, starting with direct comparisons ('heavier', 'longer'), moving on to non-standard units (e.g. handspans) and gradually introducing equipment such as scales and rulers. In developing young children's scientific observation skills, we need to remember that observing has a strong cognitive element (Nicholls 1999) – what we see is determined by what we know. Children may consider different aspects of an object important from adults (e.g. focus on a part of a flower that 'looks like a face' rather than the anther and stigma) or bring in other information (e.g. stereotyped representations from computer 'clip art'). While we may wish to draw children's attention to particular features that we consider of interest, it is important not to override their more imaginative approaches to observation. Scientific observation can be about the whole shape, form or outline of an object, not just specific details. It is also not just about looking; there should be opportunities for children to explore tactile properties and use their other senses (with due regard for health and safety considerations!) The following checklist may be helpful in setting up observation opportunities:

- Has *each* child had the opportunity to handle or be close to the objects?
- Have the children's observations been focused by discussion?
- Is the background suitable?
- Do all the children have a good view?
- Do the children know how to use magnifying aids?
- Do you want the children to record observations through drawing or digital photographs?
- Have you provided them with appropriate media and tools for recording?
- Do you want the children to focus on a particular aspect (visual element) such as colour, texture, form, pattern?
- Do you want the children to 'dissect' the objects?
- Would a 'window frame' be a useful aid to move the focus away from the overall shape of a large specimen?
- How will you develop the observations – word banks/question banks/further exploration . . . ?

Putting thinking skills together – 'playing the scientist game'

Once children have had plenty of experience of guided and structured exploration, we can begin to 'scaffold' their planning of a scientific enquiry by 'playing the scientist game' (Siraj-Blatchford and MacLeod-Brudenell 1999). If children can take on the roles of scientists – while avoiding stereotyped accessories such as white coats – they are more likely to become engaged with the enquiry and see it as relevant to their lives. The scientist game then involves a set of 'rules' or steps to be followed. Goldsworthy and Feasey (1997) introduced a technique for teachers to model planning an enquiry, involving a brainstorm of factors that could be changed (variables) jotted onto Post-it notes, which children then select from and transfer to sheets which help them to structure a question, prediction, recording table and chart. Versions of this technique aimed at young children have been developed by Devon local education authority (Devon Curriculum Services 1998), using shapes or symbols to denote particular thinking skills or phases of the planning process. An example is given below:

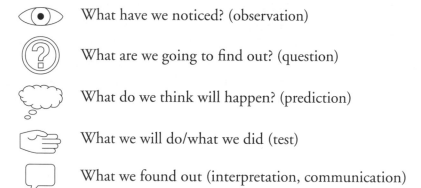

What have we noticed? (observation)

What are we going to find out? (question)

What do we think will happen? (prediction)

What we will do/what we did (test)

What we found out (interpretation, communication)

The shapes we have used for each stage are intended to convey something of what that particular thinking skill involves, which should appeal to visual learners. Other shapes can be used, but it is important to maintain consistency throughout the educational setting so children become familiar with the activity denoted by each symbol. Some teachers make a display or mobile of the shapes for the classroom, or even use giant versions on the floor for children to move between when playing the scientist game. 'I've moved to the think cloud so now I'm predicting what will happen' is a kinaesthetic way of remembering the process.

When considering the 'test' stage of the process it is important not to become too obsessed with the concept of 'fairness'. Children may well have different meanings for 'fair' from the scientific one (e.g. 'we all took turns'), and need to be shown and participate in several 'unfair' tests before they begin to see the need to change one variable while keeping others the same. Goldsworthy and Feasey's Post-its can help with this (you transfer one variable to 'we will change . . .' and all the others to 'we will keep these the same'), but so will a teacher's (or a glove puppet's) demonstration of patently unfair tests, such as dropping objects from very different heights or throwing one while dropping another. Children are often better at spotting a 'mistake' than planning a fair test themselves. They should, of course, be as fully involved in actually carrying out the test as possible, which will provide further opportunities for discussing fairness. Recording may be best done initially by an adult scribing children's comments as the enquiry proceeds (perhaps in a floorbook – see Chapter 5), though children can be invited to draw what they see happening or stick symbols onto a table or pictogram. This will begin to introduce them to the idea that scientists can record and present data in different ways.

Talking about what we have found out is probably the most important phase of the scientist game, yet is sometimes neglected through lack of time or the stress of tidying up. Harlen (1996) places great importance on speech as reflection upon what we have learned; we often understand better when we try to explain to others. Children in role as scientists can be asked to give their 'report' to an adult or a small group of peers, though we need to balance this more formal situation with opportunities for them to simply chat about the enquiry among themselves. Another way for children towards the end of Key Stage 1 to communicate their findings is to tell or write a story about them, as in the following case study set, once again, within a literacy context.

Case study: Materials from traditional tales

Mandi Macey, Year 2 class teacher at Broad Chalke CE First School, Wiltshire, describes her science work using traditional stories:

'I looked at a selection of traditional stories and thought about how they could be linked to the science concepts (about materials). In this way the content became the vehicle for the skills and concepts I wanted to teach . . . I decided that I needed to teach some science concepts first, discrete from the literacy work on traditional stories, and vice-versa. Nevertheless, I had to first teach the children to name, describe and sort a variety of materials so there were obvious links with literacy from the start. I started with the story "The Snow Queen" and linked this to the origin of ice and its properties. We investigated the different properties of water; in the words of one child:

> *"We put ice cubes into a kettle and turned it on and it melted into water and the water turned into water vapour. Then we got a metal spoon and put it against the water vapour and it turned into water again because we cooled it down and we could turn it back into ice again if we freeze it."*

'This was recorded in the form of a flow diagram and led to thinking about ice as a suitable material for making a palace. For our enquiry we chose different conditions for melting ice balloons, using a scaffolding sheet (writing frame) to develop the scientific skills of prediction, testing and drawing conclusions. This sheet had the following headings:

- *Where do you think the ice balloon will melt the most quickly? (predict)*
- *What can we do to find out where the ice will melt most quickly? (test)*
- *What happened? Why did it melt so quickly there? (interpret)*

'We try to teach the enquiry process as a formula and say it as a whole class. To communicate their findings from the enquiry, and to reinforce their understanding of the properties of ice and water, children wrote a story setting for "The Snow Queen", describing the palace and where it needed to be situated in order to stay frozen. This was made more real to the children by the presence of ice outside which we could go and observe or bring into the classroom – it was January.

'The topic moved on to other traditional tales; the story of "Hansel and Gretel" led us to investigate changes in materials involved in the process of making bread. We also discussed which other materials would have made a better trail than bread because they are more durable. We had previously investigated the strength of different materials. Now we tested hair to find out how strong it really was. The Rapunzel test involved putting a single hair in a vice and suspending a pot from it. Weights were added to the pot until the hair finally snapped.'

Commentary

Mandi and her colleagues at Broad Chalke CE First School have a systematic way of introducing children to the procedures of scientific enquiry, from a simple two-stage 'predict–test' model to one involving children in explanation of what they have seen – the first stage in forming hypotheses. They embed all their science work within a literacy context since they are convinced of the fundamental role language plays in children's scientific development. Mandi was also able to use chance occurences (e.g. icy weather) to enhance children's learning about materials and tap into their curiosity about natural phenomena. This is characteristic of good practice in the Early Years and has at its root a concern for the development of children's scientific attitudes, an important consideration in our interventions.

Developing young children's scientific attitudes

The Non-Statutory Guidance published with the original National Curriculum Order for science lists the following attitudes as important for children to develop in order to become 'good scientists':

- Curiosity
- Respect for evidence
- Willingness to tolerate uncertainty
- Critical reflection
- Perseverance
- Creativity and inventiveness
- Open-mindedness
- Sensitivity to the living and non-living environment
- Co-operation with others

(NCC 1989: A8)

We may consider that some of these attitudes young children already possess in abundance (e.g. curiosity) and that the net effect of the education system is to 'beat it out of them': 'For many children the instinctive need to find out is thwarted because it is not always convenient to have a child constantly asking questions, touching things and enquiring' (Johnston 1996: 95). Yet there are things that we as practitioners can do to prevent this from happening. It is often claimed that attitudes are 'caught' rather than taught, so if we as adults can demonstrate our curiosity and enthusiasm for phenomena which intrigue us (see Chapter 8), we can also show how our curiosity can be channelled into systematic enquiry. For example, we might muse aloud: 'I wonder why that train's pushing the other one away (magnetic coupling). I wonder what would happen if I turned it round.' Similarly, we need to be prepared to pick up on children's expressions of curiosity, as Angela demonstrated in the first case study of this chapter. Generally, reinforcing scientific attitudes through praise and expressions of interest can have a positive impact on this aspect of children's scientific development.

Other attitudes that do not come so naturally to young children can also be modelled by adults. To make a point of revealing that our own ideas have changed, for instance, can have a significant impact on children's willingness to change their ideas (Harlen 1996). For example, 'I used to think that wrapping ice up would make it melt more quickly, but now I realise that it helps keep the ice cold, because the warmth can't get in so easily.' The way we structure activities can also have an influence on whether children develop attitudes such as perseverance: 'Activities should not be so difficult that children cannot see a way forward and give up' (Johnston 1996: 100). If children lack 'ownership' of the activities they undertake, they are less likely to have respect for the evidence that comes out of them, since they are effectively testing the teacher's hypothesis, rather than their own. This further emphasises the need for free and guided exploration, in addition to any teacher-initiated enquiry we might pursue.

Summary

In this chapter we have explored the types of activity that can provide rich opportunities for us to intervene in children's scientific learning, including play, guided or structured exploration, designing and making, moving towards more systematic enquiries in Key Stage 1. Each type of activity has its strengths in helping children to gain confidence or acquire specific expertise; it is our professional judgement that needs to determine the best context to provide and most appropriate form of intervention. This might include careful questioning to elicit children's ideas (conceptual understanding); suggestions for actions they might take to move the activity forwards (often involving the exercise of scientific process skills) and modelling of appropriate scientific attitudes. In the next chapter we consider how to intervene in order to maximise children's development of design and technology capability.

CHAPTER 10

Design & technology in Key Stage 1

Dan Davies and Alan Howe

Purpose of this chapter

Through reading this chapter, you will gain

- ideas for starting points and appropriate contexts for D&T activity
- an understanding of the nature of progression in designing and making
- strategies for inclusion in D&T.

Introduction

In Chapter 6 we looked at the contribution that D&T can make to children's holistic learning in the Foundation Stage. This chapter considers how we can build on this learning as children move into Key Stage 1. D&T has been a statutory part of the Key Stage 1 National Curriculum since 1990 (DES/WO 1990) and primary practitioners have put a great deal of effort into implementing the subject requirements as it has evolved through a number of versions (Davies 2000). The current curriculum requirements are introduced with a powerful rationale for why design & technology is an important part of young children's education (DFEE/QCA 1999a: 90). It emphasises that tasks need to have a clear purpose, encourage creativity and problem solving and relate to children's wider experiences of technology in their lives, often by starting with evaluation of the made world. In making the link with the Foundation Stage it is acknowledged that teachers will be building on children's prior experiences:

> During key stage 1 pupils learn how to think imaginatively and talk about what they like and dislike when designing and making. They build on their early childhood experiences of investigating objects around them. They explore how familiar things work and talk about, draw and model their ideas. They learn how to design and make safely and could start to use ICT as part of their designing and making.
>
> (DfEE/QCA 1999a: 92)

The Programme of Study for D&T covers the following process skills:

- Developing, planning and communicating ideas
- Working with tools, equipment, materials and components to make quality products
- Evaluating processes and products

As children develop these skills, they should also be applying *knowledge and understanding of materials and components*. 'Materials' could include paper, card, wood, clay, food, textiles, construction kits and recycled objects, while 'components' refers to wheels, hinges, fastenings, buttons, food ingredients, etc. The 'Breadth of Study' section of the curriculum is brief yet important as it indicates the kinds of materials children *must* have the opportunity to work with such as 'food, items that can be put together to make products, and textiles' (DFEE/QCA 1999a: 93). This section also outlines the three types of activities that need to be included within a unit of work:

- *Investigating and evaluating a range of products (IEAs)* – when children are given the opportunity to handle and discuss products and artefacts as diverse as supermarket sandwiches or a Zimbabwean traditional cooking pot. We shall see below how this can be a powerful starting point for D&T and one way in which children can develop an understanding of the *uses and effects* of technology.
- *Focused practical tasks (FPTs)* can be thought of as short teaching inputs on a particular technique such as measuring and cutting in half, or stitching a hem to stop fraying, or element of knowledge, such as understanding of sliding mechanisms (see Chapters 5 and 8).
- *Design-and-make assignments (DMAs)* require children to engage in a holistic process of designing and making for a particular purpose from start to finish.

The National Curriculum does not tell teachers *how* to teach D&T, but we also have the QCA/DfEE scheme of work (QCA/DfEE 1998b) used in many primary schools (Ofsted 2001b), together with supporting publications such as the Design and Technology Association Helpsheets (DATA 1999b) and Lesson Plans (2002). Teachers in Key Stage 1 have broadly welcomed this guidance. The scheme of work gives detail of possible projects or 'units of work', each of which is intended to occupy 8–12 hours of curriculum time. It is recommended that one such unit is taught in each term of the Key Stage – giving six in total – to ensure that each child receives a balanced experience of different materials and knowledge of components.

The scheme of work is not a complete answer to the delivery of the subject and teachers will need the support of subject leaders in making professional judgements about adopting and adapting the scheme, considering the following factors:

- *Time allocation* – Does the current school planning allow sufficient time for each unit and activity to be taught?
- *Opportunities for cross-curricular links* – Are there opportunities to link D&T with units from other subjects in order to make a more coherent experience for

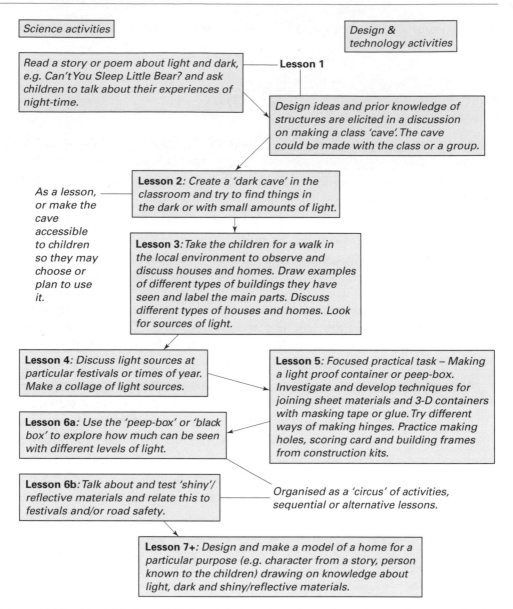

Science activities

Read a story or poem about light and dark, e.g. Can't You Sleep Little Bear? and ask children to talk about their experiences of night-time.

Design & technology activities

Lesson 1

Design ideas and prior knowledge of structures are elicited in a discussion on making a class 'cave'. The cave could be made with the class or a group.

As a lesson, or make the cave accessible to children so they may choose or plan to use it.

Lesson 2: Create a 'dark cave' in the classroom and try to find things in the dark or with small amounts of light.

Lesson 3: Take the children for a walk in the local environment to observe and discuss houses and homes. Draw examples of different types of buildings they have seen and label the main parts. Discuss different types of houses and homes. Look for sources of light.

Lesson 4: Discuss light sources at particular festivals or times of year. Make a collage of light sources.

Lesson 5: Focused practical task – Making a light proof container or peep-box. Investigate and develop techniques for joining sheet materials and 3-D containers with masking tape or glue. Try different ways of making hinges. Practice making holes, scoring card and building frames from construction kits.

Lesson 6a: Use the 'peep-box' or 'black box' to explore how much can be seen with different levels of light.

Lesson 6b: Talk about and test 'shiny'/reflective materials and relate this to festivals and/or road safety.

Organised as a 'circus' of activities, sequential or alternative lessons.

Lesson 7+: Design and make a model of a home for a particular purpose (e.g. character from a story, person known to the children) drawing on knowledge about light, dark and shiny/reflective materials.

Figure 10.1: Combining D&T and science units of work – an interactionist approach

the children and make more efficient use of curriculum time? See Figure 10.1 for an example of a unit of work linked closely to science.

- *Children's prior experiences and realistic expectations* – Does the unit build on what the children have actually done in the past? Ofsted (2001b) report that many schools have reduced the amount of D&T taught in recent years to accommodate the demands of numeracy and literacy but not re-planned the subject to account for this.

- *Relevance of contexts* – The units of work cannot be guaranteed to interest all children across the country. Each teacher will need to make judgements based on their knowledge of their own class and school as to whether there are better ways to contextualise D&T units in order to make them more relevant to local circumstances.

Getting going: Starting points for D&T

There have been many debates about what the 'D&T process' looks like, where it starts and where it finishes. We have referred to different models in Chapters 1, 2 and 8, but it is worth noting here that the value of a 'cyclical' or 'interactive' model of D&T is that it can be entered at any point. We will now discuss ways in which 'breaking in' to such a process at various points can motivate teachers and effective learning can ensue.

Starting by thinking about the needs and wants of others

During the Foundation Stage, children will have worked towards the early learning goal of 'building and constructing with a wide range of objects, selecting appropriate resources, and adapting their work where necessary' (QCA/DfEE 2000: 90). When designing and making, the outcomes will be driven by what it was *they* wanted to achieve. As discussed in Chapter 2, without significant scaffolding young children find it very difficult to think beyond their own needs and wants. For example, the children in the autumn of Year 1 at St Philip's Primary School, Bath, carried out a design-and-make assignment to make a sandwich that they would like to eat. The starting point was, therefore, a discussion about their own preferences. Their teacher had judged that it would be too demanding for them to think of the needs of others while, at the same time, meeting the requirements to plan before making and remembering safe and hygienic practices. Later in the year, when the children were more secure with the notion of designing and making, she 'scaffolded' their transition from egocentricity to awareness of the perspectives of *others* during work on playgrounds. The class went to look at a playground as starting point for thinking about the equipment different age groups would like and where a playground should be sited so as not to offend residents.

At Key Stage 1 'others' can include friends, other children in the school, their parents, carers and teachers, storybook and fantasy characters, in fact, anyone that children can easily relate to or empathise with. In Chapter 9 we saw how children in Newbridge Infant School, Bath, were motivated to make a dark cave for the little bear in *Can't You Sleep Little Bear?* There is a wide range of children's fiction books that offer good starting points for D&T because a character has a clear need or want (see Table 4.1).

Starting from a collection of designed objects

Most QCA units of work start with an IEA – examining a collection, for example of puppets or sandwiches. The advantages of this strategy are that it provides children with new knowledge (e.g. about how puppets move, or how ingredients can be combined) and suggests to them ideas for their own work. By looking at a range of products it is less likely that children will think that they have to 'copy' an idea. It may be that that looking at professionally made examples creates daunting expectations. However, in our experience children have not been put off, but rather excited and stimulated by the prospect of making something 'like' the product they have examined. A further strength of this approach is that it mirrors the approach some designers adopt when developing a new product: he or she may collect together a range of what exists in the current market and try to improve upon them or find a new market niche.

Starting with making

A third way of starting design and technology is to break into the cycle at the 'making' stage. Young children will usually do this readily; one only needs to provide access to materials for them to work with and their creativity will take them on a journey of discovery. Every Early Years classroom will provide children with access to paper, card, scrap materials, scissors and glue; by observing what they do with basic resources, teachers can use the children's ideas as starting points. Sometimes they can get 'stuck' and return again and again to making the same limited range of things. To move children on we can intervene in a number of ways:

- by introducing a new set of materials
- by sharing a child's ideas with the rest of the class
- by showing a new technique for cutting, joining or combining.

In Moorlands Infants School, Bath, Year 2 teacher, Alison Stubbs, began a design-and-make assignment by setting her class a set of challenges with a range of electrical components – batteries, wires, bulbs and buzzers. The challenges were to 'make a noise' (buzzers), 'light it up' (bulbs) and 'get-in-a-spin' (motors). This science-related making introduced children to new knowledge and skills that were then applied in a DMA to make a Christmas card that incorporated a circuit.

Starting from construction kits

Construction kits are a further 'material' likely to stimulate children's making. However, the above comments about 'moving on' children's ideas can also apply. For example, a 'craze' for making vehicles can become a stilted response after a while. A teacher can work with a group or class to show alternative ways of assembling components, or better still get a child to demonstrate. Older children might be employed to write instructions or produce designs for younger children to follow. Construction kits can also be used to 'model' ideas in three dimensions that can be made using other materials; they can also be combined with other materials to extend the range of products possible, for example adding string and card to 'Mobilo' will allow children to make models of playground equipment with it.

The nature of progression in design & technology

The ways in which children progress in D&T are perhaps less well understood and documented than any other area of the curriculum, partly because of comparatively recent developments in the subject. We can gain hints about the general nature of this progression from the Teachers' Guide to the National Scheme of Work (QCA/DfEE 1998b) and some authors cover skills progression (e.g. Bold 1999). However, we argue for a broader view, encompassing the procedural, conceptual and attitudinal elements of children's learning emphasised throughout this book. This is what Table 10.1 is intended to provide, including an idea of progression in the types of contexts within which children might undertake D&T activity, as discussed above.

Of course, this can only provide a generalised picture; children will move along the continuum implied by the 'from . . . to' statements in Table 10.1 at different stages, and progression within the different components will affect each other, for example, if children are using an unfamiliar material, they are unlikely to exercise the same degree of control in the use of cutting tools. We will now look at some of these aspects in more detail, suggesting ways in which practitioners might support some of the strands of progression indicated in Table 10.1.

Motor skills

Fine motor skills might be called 'making skills' in D&T, although this introduces an unhelpful separation between designing and making. They are parts of what Johnsey (1997) calls 'practical capability'. He refers to this as one layer of a 'toolbox' which children can build up over their educational experience, so that they have a wide range of techniques to draw upon in response to new D&T situations or design briefs. The way in which practitioners can help children add new 'tools' to their box (and 'sharpen' existing ones!) is to introduce challenges in a structured sequence, moving from materials or techniques requiring relatively basic motor skills to those which demand a high degree of accuracy and co-ordination. For example, Siraj-Blatchford and MacLeod-Brudencll (1999: 94) suggest the following sequence of materials to be introduced in order to develop children's moulding skills:

> dry sand > damp sand > playdough > plastic/wet clay > bread dough > plasticene > papier mâché

Similarly, to encourage progression in hole-making skills, they suggest the following sequence, to which we have added some more resistant materials at the end:

> thin paper > thick paper > thin card > card tubes > thin plastic bottles > thicker card > yoghurt pots > thick plastic bottles > corrugated plastic/cardboard > wood

When considering the order in which we should introduce specific tools to make these holes, it is important to 'encourage the development of a stronger grip and application

Table 10.1: General features of progression in D&T from Foundation to Key Stage 1

From . . .	To . . .
Context	
. . . familiar, simple or self-directed contexts (e.g. my teddy)	. . . less familiar, more complex or teacher-directed contexts (e.g. our playground)
Motor skills (physical development)	
. . . first encounters with simple tools for cutting, shaping and joining light materials (e.g. scissors, Pritt Stick, paper or light card, fabric, playdough, bread)	. . . more accurate use of a wider range of tools for cutting, shaping, joining and finishing materials including resistant ones (e.g. wood, plastic)
Thinking skills (designing skills)	
. . . evaluation based on simple, personal criteria (e.g. 'I like it')	. . . evaluation based on a wider range of less subjective criteria (e.g. How well does it work? How has it been joined/fastened?)
. . . designs based on personal needs and wants (e.g. 'I want to make a fire engine')	. . . designs for others as well as themselves (e.g. a home for a story character)
. . . ideas communicated through egocentric speech (commentary) e.g 'I'm sticking this on here'	. . . ideas communicated through speech, sketches, annotated parts of drawings or simple models (e.g. construction kits)
. . . planning, reviewing and changing designs as they go along, without articulating reasons	. . . a more deliberate approach to modification (e.g. 'I'm changing this bit because . . . ')
Conceptual understanding	
. . . experience of tactile and some physical characteristics of a few materials (e.g. paper can be crumpled, felt feels soft)	. . . understanding of the physical characteristics and uses of a wider range of materials (e.g. choosing to make a waterproof hat from polythene)
. . . experience of a few simple mechanisms (e.g. hinges in a flap-up book)	. . . understanding and use of a wider range of mechanisms (e.g. making moving pictures using levers and sliders)
Attitudes/values	
. . . interest in objects made by people from different cultures (e.g. textiles)	. . . respect for the skills and design ingenuity of different peoples (e.g. in looking at a range of musical instruments)
. . . working alongside other children in D&T	. . . working collaboratively with others
. . . persevering with help and encouragement	. . . persevering for longer with more independence and reflection

of pressure appropriate to the child's physical development' (Siraj-Blatchford and MacLeod-Brudenell 1999: 95). With this in mind, they suggest the sequence:

single hole punch > paper drill > tapered reamer > hand drill

It is important, for health and safety reasons, to use the right tools for the job; for example, scissors are not appropriate for making holes because of the risk of slipping or puncturing fingers. The following sequence of activities could be used to develop children's cutting skills:

cutting paper with scissors > cutting card or plastic with snips > cutting card tubes and thin wood with a junior hacksaw

As well as increasing resistance it is important to encourage children to develop the accuracy with which they can cut materials, through providing increasingly complex shapes and demonstrating how to cut around them roughly before approaching the fine detail. To make further progress in their cutting and shaping skills, we can introduce children to simple equipment for use with food, for example, at Old Sodbury Primary School in South Gloucestershire Year 1 children then applied the techniques they had been shown in a focused practical task (FPT) to shape fruit and vegetables using different tools. As they worked, they described the effects of slicing, grating and squeezing upon the fruit and vegetables, while their teacher introduced words such as 'squash', 'shred' and 'juice' to support their learning (Figure 10.2). Afterwards they recorded their activity in drawings to help them remember the techniques for when they would need to use them in designing and making fresh fruit and vegetable salads.

For children to develop joining skills we can provide sticky tape dispensers to help them 'find the end', demonstrate the extent to which retractable glue sticks should be extended and show techniques for spreading PVA evenly and thinly with a spreader. DATA (1998b) suggests the following sequence for introducing fastenings between materials:

long treasury tags > large paper binders > shorter treasury tags > large paper fasteners > short treasury tags > short paper binders and fasteners > elastic treasury tags > pipecleaners > string (threaded through hole and secured with masking tape to avoid knot tying)

To help children practise these techniques and use a range of fastenings in one piece of work, Young (1991) asked them to make 'washing lines' to which each cut out item of clothing was attached using a different fastening. When joining fabrics using thread, we can support children's progression from plastic needles to sharper steel needles with smaller eyes. For example, Moira Hill, design & technology subject leader at Elm Park Primary School, Winterbourne, wanted to build on the sewing skills her Year 1/2 class had acquired during the previous term by undertaking the QCA design & technology unit 2b 'Puppets'. With a mixed-age class she anticipated that some younger children would need additional support with stitching, so mixed

Figure 10.2: Developing vegetable grating skills

the groups for fine motor control and had them working one at a time with an adult helper while the rest of the class were developing their scripts. Figure 10.3 shows Moira supporting 'Charlie' in stitching the two felt halves of his puppet together. He gained in confidence through the activity and subsequently acted as narrator for his group's performance.

Construction kits also offer opportunities to develop children's joining and fastening skills. Most kits commonly available in Early Years settings encourage accuracy in push-fitting, for which we suggest the following sequence to provide increasing challenge:

Sticklebricks > Mobilo > Lego Duplo > Lasy > First Gear > Polydron

In addition, some kits, such as Duplo Toolo, Briomec and Bau Play feature nuts and bolts as an extension to children's 'toolkit' of fastening techniques and motor skills.

Figure 10.3: Moira supports 'Charlie' in stitching the two halves of the puppet together

Thinking skills – procedural understanding

We now come to those cognitive components of process that we have called 'thinking skills' (or 'designing skills' if you want to separate them from making). These constitute the second layer of Johnsey's 'toolbox' (1997, see above). Based upon a literature survey and classroom observations, he identifies a list of what he terms 'procedural skills' used by pupils from Nursery to Key Stage 2 as they design and make:

> *Investigating* and exploring the design context
> *Identifying needs*, opportunities and potential for design-and-make tasks
> *Clarifying* the implications of the design-and-make task
> *Specifying* criteria for judging the outcome of the design-and-make task
> *Carrying out research* into the problem and its solution
> *Generating ideas* for a product which will provide a solution
> *Modelling ideas* as a preparation for making
> *Planning and organising* the making of a product
> *Making* the product
> *Evaluating* various aspects of the process and the product as work proceeds
> *Evaluating* the final product and processes used against original criteria.
>
> (Johnsey 1997: 202)

This is an extensive list and not one we can hope to address comprehensively within this chapter. However, Johnsey makes it clear that children only use *selections* from these skills in a particular D&T activity in a random way:

> Each pupil will develop a personal set of strategies for each section of the toolbox and learn to use these in different ways. The teacher's job will be to enable the pupil to develop:
> (i) a wide range of these 'tools' for each compartment of the box
> (ii) a range of appropriate ways in which to combine these tools depending on the context and circumstances of each design task.
>
> (Johnsey 1997: 203)

To develop young children's procedural understanding, it is not appropriate to set up a rigid sequence of these skills through which they have to work. Designing is an iterative process moving backwards and forwards between activities 'inside' and 'outside the head' (Kimbell *et al.* 1991; see Figure 2.1); so it is appropriate for children to employ procedures in different orders. It is important for us to help them recognise their 'cognitive style' in designing – small steps or giant leaps, convergent or divergent thinking – to progress from random to more systematic choices of thinking skill, depending on the task.

We can certainly help children to progress in their use of individual thinking skills by providing a range of types of scaffolding (see the introduction to this chapter) including prompts. For example, to support the skill of investigating (and observing) design contexts, Johnsey (1997) suggests the following set of questions:

- What are we looking at?
- What is the purpose of each part of it?
- What might it be made of?
- What shapes can you see?
- How do they fit together?
- Is it natural, or has it been made?
- How is it different from/the same as other . . . ?

We can also support investigation by encouraging children to sort and classify. For example in the food activity referred to above, once children had observed the fruit and vegetables provided using a range of senses (sight, touch, smell, taste), class teacher Julia Sutcliffe asked them to make groups according to different criteria: by shape, hardness, whether they were eaten raw or cooked. Some children required extra support with this activity since they were unfamiliar with many of the fruit and vegetables in their unprocessed state. The children next drew the inside and outside of fruit and vegetables cut in half, giving them an appreciation of structure and texture.

To develop children's research skills, we can provide them with information in readily accessible forms. Julia Sutcliffe had provided fruit and vegetable information leaflets from the local supermarket, health centre and hospital, from which the children cut out photographs and assembled their own collage (a sort of 'virtual' salad).

To support their planning for making, Julia showed them how to write instructions which could be used to tell someone else how to make their salads, including some of the shaping words introduced during the FPT.

Modelling ideas is a thinking skill with a high cognitive content, closely related to the activity of imaging 'in the mind's eye'. Children can be helped to bring their ideas 'outside the head' using mouldable materials such as plasticene or construction kits, which can feed fresh ideas into the mental image or help to resolve technical problems. Some kits lend themselves to modelling particular types of project, for example 'Mobilo' is useful for mechanisms involving hinges, whereas 'Briomec' could be used for levers and 'First Gear' for gears. 'Polydron' is useful for modelling 'shell' structures such as packaging, while 'Tactic' is more appropriate to frameworks such as playground equipment.

Problem solving is a thinking skill that has received much attention over the years. The extent to which it is generic or transferable is debatable (if you can solve mathematical problems, it does not necessarily mean you can solve design problems) but its importance in D&T is profound. This does not mean that we should be setting children artificial 'problems' (for example, 'build a tower to support a marble') but we do need to support them in developing strategies that will help them in the midst of designing and making. The types of problem-solving strategies commonly used by children aged 4 to 7 working in groups have been studied longitudinally by C. Roden (1999: 22), who concluded that: 'the groups of children in the study used very similar types of strategies, even though they were of a different age, from different schools and engaged in different tasks'. Roden goes on to develop a taxonomy of such strategies (1999: 23), including *personalisation*, in which 'children sought to relate the task to themselves and make links with past personal experiences of a similar nature. This appeared to aid concept building and helped them bridge the gap between personal and school knowledge.' Another useful strategy was *negotiation and reposing the task*, meaning that 'children tested the boundaries of the task and what was "allowed" within the classroom culture'. In considering progression, she notes that there is a complex age-related variation in the duration, frequency and extended use of these strategies.

One way in which we can support children in their development of problem solving is to make the strategies they are using more explicit through questioning. This will promote 'self-knowledge', or 'metacognition', widely regarded as essential if you want to get better at something (see Chapter 2). For example, during an activity to design and make homes for story characters, Sarah Stillie, Year 1 teacher at Bromley Heath Infants' School, Bristol, gathered the children on the carpet for a joint problem-solving session. Each pair had to present their progress and discuss their problems – plus the ways in which they had tried to overcome them – with the wider group, who made suggestions about the way forward.

Evaluation has many roles in D&T. As indicated in Johnsey's list of procedural skills above, children can evaluate both their final outcomes and the processes they used to achieve them. Evaluating objects others have made can also raise children's awareness of design issues they may well not have considered previously: 'An awareness of ergo-nomics and anthropometrics: design which takes into account body size and handling qualities, may begin with a child exploring and talking about whether a toy feels good, how it fits in the hand, how easy it is to pick up' (DATA 1998b: 22). When consider-ing their own outcomes, young children may initially volunteer an uncritical response – 'I like it' – or one that closes down any possibility of having to work further on it: 'I wouldn't change anything.' Children may misinterpret the invitation to evaluate progress, perhaps thinking of it in behavioural terms ('I didn't muck about'). DATA (1998) offer the following set of prompts to extend children's evaluating skills:

- Do I like it? What is it that I particularly like? Focus on specifics, for example, how it moves, how it is fastened, its appearance.
- Is it what I need? Why? What purpose does it serve? How does it work?
- Is it the right size for my needs? How do I know?
- Is it strong? Does it need to be? Why?
- Is it safe? Does it need to be? Why?

(DATA 1998b: 23)

Conceptual understanding

Conceptual understanding forms the third layer in Johnsey's 'toolbox' of D&T competency (see above). As outlined in Chapter 8, we consider the main aspects of conceptual understanding in Early Years D&T to relate to the characteristics of materials and knowledge about mechanisms and control. With regard to the first of these, Siraj-Blatchford and MacLeod-Brudenell (1999: 94) suggest the following general approach to build progression in understanding:

- teach children to recognise a wide range of natural and manufactured materials
- show the importance of each material in everyday life
- provide opportunities for children to explore the qualities and characteristics of each of the different materials.

An activity that can form a valuable part of this approach is 'the materials game' described here by Young (1991: 14):

Samples of different textiles are distributed to groups of two or three children around the circle. Each group tries to think of two or three adjectives which apply to their sample. These adjectives are recorded on cards in front of each group for the whole circle to see. Each group is then asked to select a word from another group which might apply to their sample. In this way the children will begin to identify similarities and differences between the samples, which can then be used with the words to create a wall display.

This activity could of course equally well serve as a scientific introduction to the properties of materials, but as we have emphasised it is the *purpose* for which the practitioner has chosen it that makes the difference. To count as D&T – perhaps an

Figure 10.4: Sarah Stillie demonstrates hinges using the concept board

Investigation and Evaluation Activity (IEA) – it should be undertaken in preparation for a project involving designing and making with textiles, perhaps glove puppets or clothes for a teddy.

To develop children's understanding of mechanisms we need to demonstrate them in everyday objects. A collection of pop-up books, toys or kitchen implements exemplifying hinges, levers and gears can be used for a 'mechanism detective' game – how many can the children spot and name. Another approach is to make a 'concept board' showing different ways of making the same type of mechanism. For example, in the 'Homes for story characters' project, Sarah Stillie wanted to teach her class different ways of making a hinge for the opening door specified in the design brief. She made a concept board showing different methods of making a hinge, which she demonstrated and discussed with the class (Figure 10.4). Construction kits too can be used to exemplify mechanisms and mechanical control, as suggested above. The principles of electrical control (switches) are probably best taught in the context of a science lesson on circuits, for which there is guidance in Table 8.3.

Attitudes

As we have discussed in relation to science, values are probably best 'caught not taught': modelled by the practitioner and reinforced with praise. Some of the

Table 10.2: Some different kinds of values in design and technology

Values	Examples
Technical	Right materials for the job; improved performance; 'neat' solution
Economic	Thrifty use of materials/resources; maximising added value of product
Aesthetic	Pleasing to handle; attractive to look at
Social	Equality of opportunity; regard for the disadvantaged and those with disabilities
Environmental	Recycled, recyclable, biodegradable, sustainably developed
Moral	Sanctity of life
Spiritual	Commitment to a conception of humans and their relationship to nature

Source: adapted from Layton (1992: 36)

relevant attitudes are the same as those in science (open-mindedness, willingness to tolerate uncertainty, perseverance), but there are others that relate specifically to different types of D&T values (Table 10.2).

It would not be realistic to develop children's attitudes in relation to all these values, but some (such as not wasting materials) are very relevant and can be discussed with the whole class before, during or after a D&T activity. In the classroom very young children's values may be about personal likes and dislikes and it is up to the teacher to help them to recognise the basis for preferences expressed in order to help them become more open-minded. They should be made aware of the preferences of others and recognise they may be different to their own. Older children can be invited to deal with more sophisticated questions; for example at Bromley Heath Infants, Sarah Stillie chose to take advantage of the new housing development being built near the school to help children consider ways in which the development would impact upon the local community both socially and environmentally. Once the children had finished their 'Homes for story characters' she asked them to group the resulting models in a housing development – 'Fairytale land' – which considered issues of access, space and traffic (Howe *et al.* 2001).

Inclusion

We must try to ensure that we develop *all* children's learning in D&T. It is an area of the curriculum that can lend itself particularly well to inclusion, since children can follow their own interests and all achieve success at their own level. There are no right or wrong answers. However, we need to beware of practice which unintentionally excludes or disadvantages individuals or groups.

Anti-sexism

One example of an unintentional message which can be conveyed to children is that D&T is a *boys'* area of the curriculum. Emphasis upon the functional aspects of objects and models at the expense of the aesthetic, projects centred around wheeled vehicles or mechanical toys, or competitive problem-solving activities, can all convey this impression. It is important to reinforce girls' views of themselves as designers and technologists, and to value their interests as genuine D&T activities:

> Although it is well documented that girls do not use constructional and mechanical toys as often as boys, they certainly have the necessary understanding to perform competently in spatial and mechanical activities . . . Many 'female' activities (e.g. making dolls' clothes, dolls' houses, paper baskets) involve the process of conceptualizing a finished product, considering how to construct it from a range of non-specific components, executing a plan and modifying it as necessary.
>
> (Browne and Ross 1991: 50)

Although we would not advocate tailoring D&T projects to the stereotyped image of 'girls' interests', it is important to review the range of contexts within which we are setting design briefs to ensure that they have a sufficient human, social element and encourage co-operation rather than competition. Makiya and Rogers (1992) suggest that girls are more interested in tackling open-ended problems where there are value judgements to be made – an approach which will benefit boys as well. For example, thinking about how we can help Teddy visit his friends is likely to encourage more creative thinking than the brief to 'make a car'.

A particular area of gender imbalance in the D&T provision of many Early Years settings is that of construction kits, particularly if they are used as 'choosing' or 'planning' activities after children have done some 'real work'. Beat (1991) suggests a useful set of strategies for addressing the male domination of the construction area:

Strategies for involving girls with construction kits
- Store away from manufacturers' packaging – avoid stereotyped images
- Encourage children to mix kits, and add other materials
- Construction activities should be planned for and seen as important, not just something to go onto after children have finished other activities
- Encourage all children to finish their models and talk about them
- Once a model is completed, all children should be encouraged to play with it, make up a story with it
- Models should be displayed with the child's name
- Teachers and other adults need to spend time with the construction group, offering praise, encouragement and asking questions
- Have 'girls-only' times with construction kits

(adapted from Beat 1991: 83–4)

Many of the suggestions above are simply good practice in using construction kits purposefully for designing and making, so will actually benefit boys as well as girls. However, it is important that we question sexist attitudes about construction toys or any other aspect of D&T, from whomever they come. Also, since the vast majority of Early Years practitioners are female, it is the adults themselves that provide the best role models of D&T-capable women!

Anti-racism

An anti-racist teacher needs to be sensitive to the responses that children are making and be prepared to challenge inappropriate ones, for example that some children in Africa make their own toys because they 'can't afford toys like us'. Such a teacher also has to be critical of texts and resources being used to ensure that they do not carry hidden messages about 'superiority' or undervalue the achievements of those in the 'Majority World'. For example, an essential aspect of the approach to D&T advocated by the Intermediate Technology Group (Budgett-Meakin 1992) is to show parallels between the technological products and processes in the UK and elsewhere within a social, environmental and cultural context, while at the same time appreciating differences and the reasons for them. For example, a project to look at and design packaging for food products could look at the range of approaches used in different cultures, emphasising elements such as transportation and recycling.

There is also a producer–consumer relationship to consider in relation to food topics, which can be done at Key Stage 1. For example, in the fruit and vegetable project referred to earlier, class teacher Julia Sutcliffe decided to make links with the school harvest festival, which gave her the opportunity of considering wider issues with the children, such as 'Where do our fruit and vegetables come from? Do the people who grow them get a fair price? Why are some people in the world hungry?' She also decided to bring in examples such as sweet potatoes to draw the children's attention to the varied diets within our multicultural society. Old Sodbury is a small village in a predominantly white rural area, and Julia felt it important that children should begin to recognise that they were part of a larger society that includes people with different tastes and cultural backgrounds. For schools in more diverse areas that may include children with English as an Additional Language (EAL) such work can be enriched by encouraging children to provide names for the fruit and vegetables in their home languages. The visual 'language' of design (form, texture, function) is international, providing plenty of opportunities for non-verbal communication between children working together who may share few common words.

Special educational needs (SEN)

Design and technology often offers opportunities for children with particular needs to succeed and excel, not because it is 'non-academic' but because it makes use of different intelligences (spatial, interpersonal) from those valued in literacy and numeracy. The new Code of Practice for SEN (DfES 2001: para 3:18) recommends that children should be involved in their own assessment and construction of

Individual Education Plans (IEPs). Although IEPs seldom include targets for D&T we welcome this move since it builds upon the autonomous decision-taking that D&T fosters. The extra provision (Early Years Action) triggered by such IEPs can include 'extra adult time in devising the nature of the planned intervention and monitoring its effectiveness; the provision of different learning materials or special equipment; some individual or group support' (DfES 2001: para 36). Some of this could clearly be D&T-related, e.g. a child having difficulties with fine motor control might need support in holding work while he or she cuts, or even uses specially adapted scissors. Particularly relevant to D&T is the suggestion of 'play plans' in Early Years settings (e.g. for sand and water play) (White and Parry 1997: S6.17). For children with physical disabilities in classroom D&T activities, we need to list

- the physical (motor) skills required for the activity
- the aspects of the disability which are relevant to the activity
- the strengths of the pupil that can be built upon
- any modifications of the activity that might be necessary for the child.

(adapted from NCC 1991: 14)

In many cases few or no modifications will be necessary, particularly if the activity is one with a wide range of possible outcomes and no set methodology. Similarly, many of the educational needs of children with learning difficulties (as defined by Kincaid and Rapson 1983) can be met within open-ended D&T activities:

- They must succeed and be expected to succeed
- They need to understand that they make a real contribution to the work of the class
- They need to be shown what is interesting in their world
- Cognitive development must be encouraged by many varied opportunities to work with concrete materials and to use all their senses
- They need practical work to help them develop physical control
- Learning is often best organised into small steps, quickly attained, with frequent repetition and reinforcement in different guises
- Avoid written instructions and devise alternative ways of recording
- Realistic objectives need to be set
- Frequent contact with teacher, and constant encouragement, is needed.

Often some extra time spent with a supportive adult can help to ensure the experience of success in this most motivating of subject areas (see below). The motivational nature of D&T can also support children with behavioural difficulties, though we may initially wish to limit their access to potentially dangerous equipment until they have 'earned our trust' through responsible designing and making activity.

Higher attaining children

The special needs of higher attaining children, sometimes referred to as 'more able' or 'gifted', have received much attention in recent years. Such children can be identified as 'those who have the capacity to learn at a pace and level of complexity that is significantly advanced of their age peers in any domain or domains' (Porter 1999: 33, cited in Coates and McFadden 2002: 34). Again, higher attainment is rarely identified in specific relation to D&T. We can think of children with a particular creative flair, those who think 'out of the box' or who possess particular technical expertise or fine motor skills. They can sometimes be referred to by teachers as 'loners' or slightly 'unusual', but there are also those who are particularly skilled at working creatively in collaboration with others. In considering the types of provision for these children we need to choose between 'outcome-based' (e.g. harder sums) and process-based models (Coates and McFadden 2002) in which 'higher level abilities and talents are identified, and these are used as the basis for enrichment work where the emphasis, is on experiencing a range of activities and using and applying concepts learned' (p. 35). The general aim is to provide activities that are both broader and more intense, promoting higher order thinking through perhaps problem-solving challenges (though not of the art-straw tower variety!). A more specific set of criteria for extension activities is provided by Porter (1999):

> Activities that:
> - encourage higher level thinking skills such as analysis, synthesis, evaluation and problem solving
> - allow children to pursue their own interests to a depth that satisfies them
> - involve less repetition and a faster pace than usual for their age
> - promote intellectual risk-taking – that is, creativity – and divergent thinking
> - offer a high degree of complexity and variety in their content process and product.
>
> (cited in Coates and McFadden 2002: 41)

For example, in an activity to design and make moving pictures, we might invite some children to explore a wider range of mechanisms in pop-up books and produce their own book (individually or collaboratively) about a topic of their choice with a range of moving parts.

Making good use of classroom assistants

All children, when engaged in practical activities such as D&T, can benefit enormously from there being an adult around to help and guide them. Ofsted (2001b) have observed that in many schools where pupils' achievement is high, teachers make good use of classroom assistants and adult volunteers to help in D&T lessons. In an increasing number of schools, teachers prepare short written guidance notes or demonstrations for classroom assistants and parent-helpers so as to ensure consistency in approach, and that learning objectives are achieved (see Table 7.5).

Classroom assistants can help by:

- listening to the children
- talking to the children

- encouraging children to organise and manage their workspace
- ensuring that children are clear about the requirements of a task
- helping all children to participate to their full potential
- reporting back to the class teacher to aid evaluation and assessment.

The last point highlights the fact that *two-way* communications between classroom assistants and staff is vital. The teacher needs to be aware of an assistant's particular skills and areas of expertise. Classroom assistants need to be as clear as the children about the teacher's expectations. In D&T it is important that there is no misunderstanding about why the children are engaged in an activity – is the process or the product more important? For example, a classroom assistant may believe that the teacher requires a neat and tidy end product, whereas the teacher wants children to explore the materials in an open ended way to solve their own problems.

Being an assistant in someone else's classroom can be a rather daunting task. On an in-service course, a group of subject leaders from South Gloucestershire schools were asked to think of some common problems faced by classroom assistants. Many of the problems identified related to children's comments. They were then asked to suggest how to deal with them. These are some of their suggestions:

(Child:) *'Can you do this for me?'*
The answer should certainly be 'no'. Help the child by considering whether the task can be broken down into more manageable steps. Perhaps the child doesn't know where to start. Some exploration may be needed. Talk to the child about their ideas. Demonstrate a skill on a piece of scrap material and get the child to do the same.

'I've finished.' (after two minutes)
Think what it was the child was asked to do. Perhaps they have finished! If you feel they have, then can you suggest further tasks to develop the skills or concepts in question. Perhaps ask the teacher for extension ideas. More usually the child will not have concentrated on the task. They might want to get on with something else, or lack confidence in their ability. A conversation can often reveal real meaning behind what children say. The teaching assistant must have as high an expectation of each child as the teacher. You might point out to the child how she/he could develop the work – look to other children to provide suggestions. It might be better for the child to start again – do not criticise the first effort but say 'show me how you did that', or 'let us make one together'.

'Do you like it?' (and you're not sure what it is!)
Children will always want adults' approval and praise; as a general rule be positive and smile! Ask questions to encourage the child to appraise their own work. 'Can you tell me how you have made this?' 'Tell me about your work,' 'Tell me what you did first' or 'Show me what it can do' might be good opening gambits.

Expect the child to talk through the process of making the work, the materials used, the problems solved and their achievements. Remember that the teacher had learning objectives for the task. Comment on how the child has achieved these. You could begin with 'I like the way that you have . . .' and go on to mention whether the child has been thoughtful, used materials in a particular way or shown a good attitude. You might praise the perseverance shown, or the problem-solving skills exhibited.

'I can't do that.'

There could be a number of reasons why a child would make such a comment. It may mean 'I have been told I am no good.' Obviously further investigation is needed through a conversation between adult and child. This type of reason is of the most concern and will need careful and long-term handling by the class teacher. A child's self-esteem can be affected deeply by comments from adults, parents or other children. It is imperative that within the primary classroom positive comments are made about all children's achievements. You can provide a valuable audience for their work. During design & technology sessions there are plenty of opportunities to comment on what the children are doing. A teaching assistant has an equal responsibility to value and praise children's efforts. Comments such as 'I can't do that either,' or 'You're as hopeless as me!' might be well-meaning but perpetuate the idea that practical activity is something some children can do and some can't. In the primary school it should be considered that all children have the potential to succeed given opportunities, guidance and support.

In the short term the assistant will need to encourage and praise every genuine effort by the child. Comparisons with other children should be avoided. Allow the child to experiment or play with the media before committing the child. Inform the teacher of the comment so that she can use this information for future planning.

Summary

In this chapter we have followed children's learning in design & technology through from play-based experiences in the Foundation Stage to the more structured projects of Key Stage 1. We have outlined the strands of progression this entails, providing strategies for extending children's skills, knowledge and attitudes while ensuring that there is equality of access to all. This focus on D&T does not imply denial of our 'interactionist' approach to young children's education outlined in Chapter 1, as the example of a joint science and D&T unit of work (Figure 10.1) demonstrates. It is our firm belief that these areas of the curriculum continue to support each other to the benefit of children's learning well beyond the Early Years. It is our hope that through reading this book you are able to recognise and support these aspects of young children's development wherever they occur.

References

Alexander, R., Rose, J. and Woodhead, C. (1992) *Curriculum Organisation and Classroom Practice in Primary Schools: A discussion paper*. London: Department of Education and Science.

Assessment Reform Group (1999) *Assessment for Learning: Beyond the Black Box*. Cambridge: Cambridge University Press.

Athey, C. (1990) *Extending Thought in Young Children: A Parent–Teacher Partnership*. London: Paul Chapman.

Awdurdod Cymwysterau, Cwricwlwm ac Asesu Cymru (ACCAC) (2000) *Desirable Outcomes for Children's Learning before Compulsory School Age*. Cardiff: ACCAC.

Bateson, P. and Martin, P. (2000) *Design for a Life: How Behaviour Develops*. London: Jonathan Cape.

Baynes, K. (1992) *Children Designing: Learning Design*. Occasional Paper No. 1. Loughborough: Loughborough University of Technology.

Beat, K. (1991) 'Design it, build it, use it: girls and construction kits', in Browne, N. (ed.) *Science and Technology in the Early Years*, 77–90. Buckingham: Open University Press.

Berger, A. (1997) *Narratives in Popular Culture, Media, and Everyday Life*. London: Sage.

Blenkin, G. and Kelly, A. V. (eds) (1988) *Early Childhood Education: A Developmental Curriculum*. London: Paul Chapman.

Bold, C. (1999) *Progression in Primary Design and Technology*. London: David Fulton.

Browne, N. and Ross, C. (1991) 'Girls' stuff, boys' stuff: young children talking and playing', in Browne, N. (ed.) *Science and Technology in the Early Years*, 37–51. Buckingham: Open University Press.

Bruce, T. (1994) 'Play, the universe and everything!' in Moyles, J. (ed.) *The Excellence of Play*, 189–98. Buckingham: Open University Press.

Bruce, T. (1997) *Early Childhood Education*, 2nd edn. London: Hodder & Stoughton.

Bruce, T. and Meggitt, C. (1996) *Childcare and Education*. London: Hodder & Stoughton.

Bruner, J. S. (1963) *The Process of Education*. London: Random House.

Bruner, J. S. (1990) *Acts of Meaning*. Cambridge, Mass./London: Harvard University Press

Bruner, J. S. (1996) *The Culture of Education*. Cambridge, Mass./London: Harvard University Press.

Bruner, J. S., Jolly, A. and Slyva, K. (eds) (1976) *Play: Its Role in Development and Evolution*. Harmondsworth: Penguin.

Budgett-Meakin, C. (ed.) (1992) *Make the Future Work*. London: Longman.

Chomsky, N. (1968) *Language and Mind*. New York: Harcourt Brace and World.

Coates, D. and McFadden, J. (2002) 'An evaluation of the impact of INPUT on the education of able primary children', *Journal of Design and Technology Education* 7(1), 34–42.

Claxton, G. (1998) *Hare Brain, Tortoise Mind; Why Intelligence Increases When You Think Less*. London: Fourth Estate.

Cohen, D. (2002) *How the Child's Mind Develops*. East Sussex: Taylor & Francis.

David, T. (ed.) (1999) *Teaching Young Children*. London: Paul Chapman.

Davies, D. (1996) 'Professional design and primary children', *International Journal of Technology and Design Education* 6, 45–59.

Davies, D. (1997) 'The relationship between science and technology in the primary curriculum: alternative perspectives', *Journal of Design and Technology Education* 2(2), 101–11.

Davies, D. (2000) 'Ten years of universal primary technology education in England and Wales: what have we learnt?', *Journal of Design and Technology Education* 5(1), 26–35.

Davies, D. and Allebone, B. (1998) 'Lacking the knowledge: subject expertise in the primary classroom', *Goldsmiths' Journal of Education* 1(1), 17–22.

de Boo, M. (2000) *Science 3–6: Laying the Foundations in the Early Years*. Hatfield: Association for Science Education.

Department for Education and Employment (DfEE) (1998a) *The National Literacy Strategy*. London: DfEE.

Department for Education and Employment (DfEE) (1998b) *Circular 4/98: Requirements for Courses of Initial Teacher Education*. London: DfEE.

Department for Education and Employment (DfEE) (1999) *The National Numeracy Strategy*. London: DfEE.

Department for Education and Employment (DfEE)/Qualifications and Curriculum Authority (QCA) (1999a) *The National Curriculum: Handbook for Primary Teachers in England*. London: DfEE/QCA.

Department for Education and Employment (DfEE)/Qualifications and Curriculum Authority (QCA) (1999b) *Science in the National Curriculum*. London: DfEE/QCA.

Department for Education and Employment (DfEE)/Qualifications and Curriculum Authority (QCA) (1999c) *Design and Technology in the National Curriculum*. London: DfEE/QCA.

Department for Education and Skills (DfES) (2001) *Special Educational Needs Code of Practice*. London: DfES.

Department of Education and Science (DES) (1990) *Starting with Quality: Report of the Committee of Enquiry into the Educational Experiences Offered to 4 and 5 Year Olds*. London: HMSO.

Department of Education and Science (DES)/Welsh Office (WO) (1990) *Technology in the National Curriculum*. London: HMSO.

Design and Technology Association (DATA) (1996) *The Design and Technology Primary Co-ordinators' File*. Wellesbourne: DATA.

Design and Technology Association (DATA) (1998a) *Primary School-based INSET Manual for Design and Technology: Volume 1*. Wellesbourne: DATA.

Design and Technology Association (DATA) (1998b) *The Design and Technology Handbook for Pre-school Providers*. Wellesbourne: DATA.

Design and Technology Association (DATA) (1999a) *Primary School-based INSET Manual for Design and Technology: Volume 2*. Wellesbourne: DATA.

Design and Technology Association (DATA) (1999b) *DATA Helpsheets for Year 2000 and Beyond*. Wellesbourne: DATA.

Design and Technology Association (DATA) (2002) *Lesson Plans for the QCA Design and Technology Scheme of Work*. Wellesbourne: DATA.

Design Council (1991) *Stories as Starting Points for Design and Technology*. London: Design Council.

Devon Curriculum Services – Science (1998) *Writing Frames for Investigations for KS1, 2, 3 and Beyond*. Exeter: Devon County Council.

Donaldson, M. (1978) *Children's Minds*. Glasgow: Fontana.

Donaldson, M. (1992) *Human Minds*. London: Fontana.

Dowling, M. (2002) 'The impact of stress on early development', in Fisher, J. (ed.) *The Foundations of Learning*, 41–56. Buckingham: Open University Press.

Driver, R. (1983) *The Pupil as Scientist?* Milton Keynes: Open University Press.

Edgington, M. (1998) *The Nursery Teacher in Action: Teaching 3, 4 and 5-Year-Olds*. London: Paul Chapman.

Feasey, R. (1994) 'The challenge of science', in Aubrey, C. (ed.) *The Role of Subject Knowledge in the Early Years of Schooling*, 73–88. London: Falmer.

Fensham, P. (1986) 'Science for all', *Educational Leadership* 44, 18–23.

Feyerabend, P. (1994) *Against Method: Outline of an Anarchist Theory of Knowledge*. London: Verso.

Fisher, J. (1996) *Starting from the Child? Teaching and Learning from 4 to 8*. London: Paul Chapman.

Foulds, K., Gott, R. and Feasey, R. (1992) *Investigative Work in Science: A Report Commissioned by the National Curriculum Council*. York: NCC.

Gardner, H. (1983) *Frames of Mind: The Theory of Multiple Intelligences*. London: Fontana.

Gardner, H. (1999) *The Disciplined Mind*. New York: Simon & Schuster.

Gardner, P. (1994) 'Representations of the relationship between science and technology in the curriculum', *Studies in Science Education* 24(1), 1–13.

Goldschmied, E. and Jackson, S. (1994) *People Under Three: Young Children in Day Care*. London: Routledge.

Goldsworthy, A. and Feasey, R. (1997) *Making Sense of Primary Science Investigations*, 2nd edn. Hatfield: Association for Science Education.

Gopnik, A., Meltzoff, A. and Kuhl, P. (1999) *How Babies Think*. London: Weidenfeld & Nicolson.

Greenfield, S. (2000) *Brain Story*. London: BBC Books.

Grindley, S. and Varley S. (1996) *Why Is the Sky Blue?* London: Anderson Press.

Harlen, W. (1996) *The Teaching of Science in Primary Schools*, 2nd edn. London: David Fulton.

Harlen, W. (2000) *The Teaching of Science in Primary Schools*, 3rd edn. London: Paul Chapman.

Harlen, W. and Holroyd, C. (1995) *Primary Teachers' Understanding of Concepts in Science and Technology*, Interchange No. 35. Edinburgh: SOED.

Harlen, W. and Osborne, R. (1985) 'A model for learning and teaching applied to primary science', *Journal of Curriculum Studies* 2(17), 133–46.

Harrington, D. M. (1990) 'The ecology of human creativity: a psychological perspective', in Runco, M. A. and Albert, R. S. (eds) *Theories of Creativity*, 143–69. London: Sage.

Hill, W. F. (1997) *Learning: Survey of Psychological Interpretations*, 6th edn. New York: Addison-Wesley.

Howe, L. (1990) *Collins Primary Science, Key Stage 1 Set Two: Stories*. London: Collins Educational.

Howe, A., Davies, D. and Ritchie, R. (2001) *Primary Design and Technology for the Future: Creativity, Culture and Citizenship in the Curriculum*. London: David Fulton.

Hurst, V. (1997) *Planning for Early Learning: Educating Young Children*, 2nd edn. London: Paul Chapman.

Hutt, C. (1979) 'Play in the under-fives: form, development and function', in Howells, J. (ed.) *Modern Perspectives in the Psychiatry of Infancy*, 94–144. New York: Brunner/Mazel.

Jarvis, T. and Rennie, L. (1996) 'Perceptions about technology held by primary teachers in England', *Research in Science and Technology Education* 14(1), 43–55.

Johnsey, R. (1997) 'Improving children's performance in the procedures of design and technology', *Journal of Design and Technology Education* 2(3), 201–7.

Johnston, J. (1996) *Early Explorations in Science*. Buckingham: Open University Press.

Johnston, J. and Hayed, M. (1995) 'Teachers' perceptions of science and science teaching', *European Conference on Research in Science Education, Proceedings, Leeds 1995*. Leeds: University of Leeds.

Jones, J. C. (1980) *Design Methods: Seeds of Human Futures*, 1980 edn. Chichester: John Wiley.

Karmiloff-Smith, A. (1994) *Baby It's You.* London: Ebury Press.

Kimbell, R., Stables, K., Wheeler, T., Wozniak, A. and Kelly, A. V. (1991) *The Assessment of Performance in Design and Technology.* London: Evaluation and Monitoring Unit (EMU), School Examinations and Assessment Council (SEAC).

Kincaid, D. and Rapson, H. (1983) *Science for Children with Learning Difficulties.* London: MacDonald Educational.

Kosslyn, S. M. (1978) 'Imagery and cognitive development: a teleological approach', in Seigler, R. (ed.) *Children's Thinking: What Develops?*, 74–85. New Jersey: Lawrence Erlbaum.

Kuhn, T. S. (1970) *The Structure of Scientific Revolutions.* Chicago: University of Chicago Press.

Layton, D. (1992) 'Values in design and technology', in Budgett-Meakin, C. (ed.) *Make the Future Work*, 36–53. London: Longman.

Lewisham Education and Culture (1999) *Find That Book: Making Links Between Literacy and the Broader Curriculum.* London: Lewisham Education and Culture.

Makiya, H. and Rogers, M. (1992) *Design and Technology in the Primary School.* London: Routledge.

McCormick, R., Davidson, M. and Levinson, R. (1995) 'Making connections: students' scientific undestanding of electric currents in design and technology', in Smith, J. S. (ed.) *IDATER 95*, 123–7. Loughborough: Loughborough University of Technology.

Mercer, N. (2000) *Words and Minds.* London: Routledge.

Millar, R. and Osborne, J. (1998) *Beyond 2000: Science Education for the Future.* London: King's College London, School of Education.

Mortimer, H. (2001) *Special Needs and Early Years Provision.* London: Continuum.

Moyles, J. (1989) *Just Playing? The Role and Status of Play in Early Childhood Education.* Milton Keynes: Open University Press.

National Advisory Committee on Creative and Cultural Education (NACCCE) (1999) *All Our Futures: Creativity, Culture and Education.* Suffolk: DfEE.

National Assembly for Wales (2001) *The Learning Country.* Cardiff: NAW.

National Curriculum Council (NCC) (1989) *Non-statutory Guidance: Science.* York: NCC.

National Curriculum Council (NCC) (1991) *Science and Pupils with Special Educational Needs.* York: NCC.

National Curriculum Design and Technology Working Group (1988) *Interim Report.* London: Department for Education and Science/Welsh Office.

National Healthy School Standard (2002) *A Review of Evidence of the Impact on Schools of the Implementation of the National Healthy School Standard Drawn from the Ofsted Database of Schools in England Inspected September 2000–July 2001.* London: NHSS.

Naylor, S. and Keogh, B. (1997) *Starting Points for Science.* Sandbach: Millgate House.

Naylor, S. and Keogh, B. (2000) *Concept Cartoons in Science Education*. Sandbach: Millgate House.

Nicholls, G. (1999) 'Young children investigating: adopting a constructivist framework', in David, T. (ed.) *Teaching Young Children*, 111–24. London: Paul Chapman.

Novak, J. D. and Gowin, D. B. (1984) *Learning How to Learn*. Cambridge: Cambridge University Press.

Nuffield Foundation (1993) *Nuffield Primary Science, Key Stage 1 Teachers' Guides*. London: Collins Educational.

Nutbrown, C. (1999) *Threads of Thinking*. London: Paul Chapman.

Office for Standards in Education (Ofsted) (2000) *The Quality of Nursery Education for Three and Four-Year-Olds 1999–2000*. London: Ofsted.

Office for Standards in Education (Ofsted) (2001a) *Standards and Quality in Education 1999–2000: The Annual Report of Her Majesty's Chief Inspector of Schools*. London: Stationery Office.

Office for Standards in Education (Ofsted) (2001b) *Subject Reports, 1999–2000: Primary Design & Technology*. London: Ofsted.

Ollerenshaw, C. and Ritchie, R. (1997) *Primary Science: Making It Work*. London: David Fulton.

Parkinson, E. and Thomas, C. (1999) 'Design and technology: the subject integrator', in David, T. (ed.) *Teaching Young Children*, 93–110. London: Paul Chapman.

Peacock, A. (1998) *Letts QTS Science for Primary Teachers Audit and Self-study Guide*. London: Letts.

Pearce, P. (1987) *The Tooth Ball*. Harmondsworth: Picture Puffins.

Piaget, J. (1929) *The Child's Conception of the World*. New York: Harcourt Brace.

Pinker, S. (1994) *The Language Instinct: New Science of Language and Mind*. Harmondsworth: Penguin.

Pollard, A. and Filer, A. (1999) *The Social World of Pupil Career: Strategic Biographies Through Primary School*. London: Cassell.

Porter, L. (1999) *Gifted Young Children: A Guide for Teachers and Parents*. Buckingham: Open University Press.

Qualifications and Curriculum Authority (QCA)/Department for Education and Employment (DfEE) (1998a) *Science: A Scheme of Work for Key Stages 1 and 2*. London: QCA.

Qualifications and Curriculum Authority (QCA)/Department for Education and Employment (DfEE) (1998b) *Design and Technology: A Scheme of Work for Key Stages 1 and 2*. London: QCA.

Qualifications and Curriculum Authority (QCA)/Department for Education and Employment (DfEE) (2000) *Curriculum Guidance for the Foundation Stage*. London: QCA.

Qualifications and Curriculum Authority (QCA) (2001) *Planning for Learning in the Foundation Stage*. London: QCA.

Qualifications and Curriculum Authority (QCA) (2002) *Assessment and Reporting*

Arrangements. http://www.qca.org.uk/ca/5–14/afl/definitions.asp. Last updated 11 January 2001, accessed 28 March 2002.

Ridley, M. (1999) *Genome: The Autobiography of a Species.* London: Fourth Estate.

Riley, J. and Savage, J. (1994) 'Bulbs, buzzers and batteries: play and science', in Moyles, J. (ed.) *The Excellence of Play*, 136–44. Buckingham: Open University Press.

Ritchie, R. (1995) *Primary Design and Technology: A Process for Learning.* London: David Fulton.

Ritchie, R. (2001) *Primary Design and Technology: A Process for Learning*, 2nd edn. London: David Fulton.

Robinson, K. (2001) *Out of Our Minds: Learning to be Creative.* Oxford: Capstone.

Roden, C. (1999) 'How children's problem solving strategies develop at Key Stage 1', *Journal of Design and Technology Education* 4(1), 21–7.

Roden, J. (1999) 'Young children are natural scientists', in David, T. (ed.) *Young Children Learning*, 130–55. London: Paul Chapman.

Rogoff, B. (1990) *Apprenticeship in Thinking: Cognitive Development in Social Context.* New York: Oxford University Press.

School Curriculum and Assessment Authority (SCAA) (1996) *Nursery Education: Desirable Outcomes for Children's Learning on Entering Compulsory Education.* London: SCAA/DfEE.

Shulman, L. S. (1987) 'Knowledge and teaching: foundations of the new reform', *Harvard Education Review* 7(1), 1–22.

Siraj-Blatchford, J. and MacLeod-Brudenell, I. (1999) *Supporting Science, Design and Technology in the Early Years.* Buckingham: Open University Press.

Siraj-Blatchford, I. and Siraj-Blatchford, J. (2001) 'A content analysis of pedagogy in the DfEE/QCA 2000 guidance', *Early Education* 35, 7–8.

Stevens, J. (2002) 'Windy day activities', *Practical Pre-School* 31.

Stringer, J. (1996) 'Childspeak science, level 5', *Question of Maths and Science* 2, 36–8.

Sweet, B. (1996) 'I think DT should stand for deep thinking', in Whitebread, D. (ed.) *Teaching and Learning in the Early Years*, 275–91. London: Routledge.

Tizard, B. and Hughes, M. (1984) *Young Children Learning.* London: Fontana.

Trevarthen, C. (1995) *How Children Learn Before School.* Lecture to BAECE, Newcastle University, 2 November.

von Glasersfeld, E. (1978) 'Radical constructivism and Piaget's concept of knowledge', in Murray, F. B. (ed.) *The Impact of Piagetian Theory*, 109–24. Baltimore: University Park Press.

von Glasersfeld, E. (1989) 'Learning as a constructive activity', in Murphy, P. and Moon, R. (eds.) *Developments in Learning and Assessment*, 5–18. Sevenoaks: Hodder & Stoughton.

Vygotsky, L. S. (1962) *Thought and Language.* New York: Wiley.

Wells, G. (1986) *The Meaning Makers.* London: Hodder & Stoughton.

White, M. and Parry, J. (1997) *Quality Play: A Response to Special Needs in the Group Setting.* Yeovil: National Portage Association.

Whitebread, D. (ed.) (1996) *Teaching and Learning in the Early Years*. London: Routledge.

Whitehead, M. (1997) *Language and Literacy in the Early Years*. London: Paul Chapman.

Williams, J. (2003) *Promoting Independent Learning in the Classroom*. Buckingham: Open University Press.

Wood, D. (1988) *How Children Think and Learn*. Oxford: Blackwell.

Young, N. (1991) *Signs of Design: The Early Years*. London: Design Council.

Index